WORSHIP SERVICES USING THE ARTS

Worship Services
Using the Arts

By
LOUISE H. CURRY
and
CHESTER M. WETZEL

THE WESTMINSTER PRESS
PHILADELPHIA

LIBRARY OF CONGRESS CATALOG CARD No. 61–6230

PRINTED IN THE UNITED STATES OF AMERICA

To Our Mothers
Who First Introduced Us to the Arts

CONTENTS

8

PREFACE

In preparing a book of services of worship designed for the local church, authors are put at a distinct disadvantage, for they must deal with several unknown quantities in designing these services — the physical setting, the size of the church, the needs of individuals and groups, and you, the reader. We would be the first to acknowledge that all these factors need be taken into consideration by the people who use this book, yet we also firmly believe that there is an overtone of imagination in the arts, and that persons working in this field will have the imagination to use artistically what we have presented and thus create their own services. Throughout the book we have attempted to make it clear that our suggested services are to be adapted, augmented, or abbreviated as the context of the local church requires. It is only in designing the service to meet the needs of the individual church that it can be truly meaningful.

Yet with all these unknown quantities, our experience in working with people from many churches — in summer leadership training schools and in workshops — has given us the motivation and courage to share our experiences and information, our experimentation and adaptations. In our teaching we have drawn upon the experiences we have had in our own local church settings to add authority and dimension to the ideas that we were presenting. Those who have listened to us with patience have been kind enough to ask us to keep in touch with them and send them the services that we are continually creating. In most cases, this has been impossible, so we have collected them in this way in the hope that they can be of use to many.

In preparing the services for this book, we have edited them so that there will be a minimum of rehearsal time; however, when the number of rehearsals is suggested, this is to be taken as the minimum. There may be a need for additional rehearsals, for we feel that it is important to do all in the church with a touch of excellence. We would hope, however, that the rehearsals and the sharing of the finished service with other groups would be infused with enjoyment, relaxation, and the opportunity for spiritual insight and growth.

We hope this book will find wide use among ministers, directors of Christian education, ministers of music, and all persons in the local church who are interested in the arts in worship. We have tried to keep in mind the local church and have designed the services for use in church-wide gatherings and in smaller groups, such as departmental services of worship, women's groups, and youth groups. They can also be used for youth rallys, in summer camps, vacation schools, and conferences.

If this approach to worship is new to you, or if you hesitate because there seems to be a lack of talent in the church, we urge you to reconsider. The most difficult step you will have to take is the initial decision to undertake this kind of presentation. When this decision is made, you will find that there is an abundance of talent in your congregation. With the growth of community theater groups and art associations, the talents of many people are continually being developed and expanded. It is also our hope that the arts may, in this way, be brought back into the church, and that the use of these services may be an impetus for the formation of drama groups, additional choirs, art committees, and perhaps for an annual Christian Festival of the Arts. This may be a means for the church to reach out into the community and bring members into the fellowship of the church.

We would be ungrateful if we did not pay tribute to the many people in several churches who have worked with us in preparing and presenting these services. They have given us their time and their ideas, their encouragement and their suggestions for improvement. We are particularly grateful to Dr. W. Lawrence Curry for the guidance he has given us in this venture, and to Mrs. Robert Brown and Mrs. Raymond Vermilyea for their help in typing the manuscript. We are also grateful to Mrs. Haydn Jones and Mrs. William Warren for the original material used in " ' The Miracle of the Manger,' " and to Mrs. Bernard Read for her original dramatization used in " The Continuing Christ."

And so we offer these services that have given us so much pleasure in creating and in sharing with others, with the hope that they may give you examples and incentives for your own creativity. We pray that you will keep in mind that God speaks to us in many ways and through many experiences. We should surely respond with the talents and abilities that he has given us.

LOUISE H. CURRY
CHESTER M. WETZEL

Jenkintown, Pennsylvania

SUGGESTIONS FOR BUILDING WORSHIP SERVICES

THEME	CALL TO WORSHIP	HYMNS	SCRIPTURE	ANTHEM	ART	POETRY
Adoration	Rev. 15:3, 4 "This Is the House of the Lord"[1]	"Joyful, Joyful We Adore Thee" "Praise Ye the Lord, the Almighty"	Ps. 150	"Praise the Lord, Ye Saints on High"[1] or "Blessing and Honor"[10]	St. Francis Preaching (Giotto)[7]	"Canticle of the Creatures"[5]
Thanksgiving	Ps. 95:1-7 "A Thanksgiving Antiphon"[12]	"Now Thank We All Our God" "We Plough the Fields, and Scatter"	Ps. 65	"A Thanksgiving Carol"[1] or "A Thanksgiving Antiphon"[12]	The Angelus (Millet)[8]	"Thanksgiving"[5]
God in Nature	"For the Beauty of the Earth" "Praise the Lord: Ye Heavens, Adore Him"	"My God, I Thank Thee, Who Hast Made" "The Spacious Firmament on High"	Ps. 19	"Fairest Lord Jesus" (Descant)[2] or "Lord of All Being"[12]	Peace and Plenty (Inness)[9]	"Christ Was the Outdoor Son of God"[6]
Consecration	Ps. 51:10-12 "God Be in My Head"[4][11]	"Take Thou Our Minds, Dear Lord" "'Come Unto Me, Ye Weary'"	Isa. 6:1-8 Ps. 139	"Be Thou My Vision"[10] or "Christ of the Upward Way"[12]	Praying Hands (Dürer)[3]	"Conversion" (A Dialogue)[5]

I

INTRODUCTION

" ALL CREATURES OF OUR GOD AND KING "

The worship of God by his people gathered together in a common experience has spiritually strengthened man through the centuries and has enabled him to express his thoughts and desires to God in many forms. In recent times, worship has too often been conceived of as form or ritual led by the minister with perfunctory responses by the people rather than as a common and meaningful experience on the part of the entire congregation. There must be a design or pattern to give dignity to the service of worship, but there must also be a fresh approach — a correlation of speech, music, color, and movement — to invest the common worship of God with renewed and contemporary meaning.

Worship is an interactive process. Its purpose is to bring man closer to God through the inspiration and instruction provided by his fellow men, and also to lead man to confrontation by the living God. Our worship is directed toward God, but it provides also for God's action toward men in this present age. We cannot say when this confrontation will take place; we can only set the stage. It is important that we make use of varied ways by which the individual may be inspired, taught, and ultimately confronted by God. Since common worship connotes the participation of all, it is not to be seen from the point of view of the spectator, but from the experiences of individuals as they become involved in a common experience. It is our conviction that the arts can be used effectively to provide meaningful experiences in worship, and that through speech, music, color, and movement, the worshiper can be led to a richer experience in the Christian life. Through the correlation of the arts, the outward stimulus will be translated to the inner life of the individual and help to create a new spirit within him.

The arts of the church are in the process of being rediscovered as a medium of inspiration and teaching. Speech, music, color, and movement comprise a dynamic part of the Christian life and should be used in the context of the church. They may aid in the interpretation of the Bible and the Christian life and provide a context for our contemporary faith. This does not mean that these forms need to be elaborate, for there is great power and strength in simplicity. It is more important to pay careful attention to the standards and quality of the materials used than to clothe inferior materials in an elaborate setting. Christian leaders must select the very finest in the arts to help people grow, but the finest can be used in simple presentations that will be effective in leading people to a meaningful experience of worship.

The services of worship that are included in this book are designed to show the correlation of the arts as they have been used to interpret various themes. The services are suggested patterns that may be followed by individuals in the local church, but it is hoped that they will be primarily an inspiration for the creation of other services of worship. It must be pointed out here that it is not necessarily the most polished service that is the most effective. One of the factors that must be paramount is the dedication and commitment of the persons who are planning and taking part in the service. The effectiveness of a service of worship is also conditioned both by the physical setting and by the background of experience of the congregation. Professional leaders in the local church, the minister, the minister of music, and the director of Christian education, working together and with dedicated, interested volunteer leaders, best know the needs and understanding of the members of the congregation and can create services of worship that grow out of the current experiences of individuals and groups in the church. There will be opportunities for committees of adults, young people, and children co-operatively to plan, prepare for, and participate in these services. Many of the programs described here have grown out of this co-operative planning and working together on the part of both the professional staff and the entire congregation.

The services of worship that follow may be used with a minimum of facilities. They may be presented in the church sanctuary, in the church social hall, in small meeting rooms, or out of doors, but wherever they are presented and experienced, it is hoped that they will stem from a sharing of talents and abilities and move toward the development of strength for Christian living.

"O WORSHIP THE KING ALL GLORIOUS ABOVE"

True worship is directed toward God, and no matter what devices and designs man may use, worship can be meaningful only to the extent that man worships in spirit. The services of worship that are included in the book are intended, not as ends in themselves, but as suggestions for creating experiences in worship. They are given, first in synopsis form and then in explicit detail, to generate ideas in the minds of individuals. In order to be really meaningful, they must be expanded, compressed, and changed to meet the needs of the local group. The chart of " Suggestions for Building Worship Services " (page 12) gives outlines that may be used by various groups in the church, and with adaptations could be a basis for services of worship planned by age groups from the fourth grade upward. The services of worship in the chart may serve as patterns, and the following techniques can be used to include the arts:

The *speaking choir* may read together or antiphonally the call to worship and the Scripture lesson. The choir may be used to speak the poetry that is suggested. Some of the hymns can be spoken rather than sung. The speaking of the words of a well-known hymn, in a meaningful way, can give new insight and understanding to those who listen.

The *singing choir* will traditionally sing the anthem. This choir will lead the congregation in the singing of the hymns and may sing the call to worship. The call to worship may be a hymn, or it may be an original setting of the suggested Scripture, composed by the choir especially for the service. To combine the sung and spoken parts, the speaking choir could read a portion of a poem and the singing choir could respond with a hymn stanza conveying a similar meaning. The poem " Canticle of the Creatures," for example, could be interspersed with stanzas from the hymn " All Creatures of Our God and King "[13] set to the hymn tune " Lasst uns erfreuen."

Color can be used through reproductions of great art, either by displaying a picture on the worship table, by projecting a slide, or by posing a picture. Various emphases in the service of worship can be achieved by the use of light, with softer and more subdued light creating a feeling of meditation, and heightened, more intense light and color creating a feeling of exultation.

The use of *rhythmic movement* is not often a part of worship in the Christian church; yet there are great possibilities for this medium in interpretation of the message of the church. Rhythmic movement is part of our heritage and was used by the Hebrews in worship. It may be effectively used in present-day worship to interpret ideas presented through poetry, narration, hymns, or Scripture.

Many times during the church year a short service of worship is needed to precede a special program. These services do not have to be prosaic or stereotyped, but can take on new meaning through the use of the arts. In specifying the various media in the chart of " Suggestions for Building Worship Services (page 12)," it has been our purpose to give patterns that may be followed in your own services of worship, emphasizing our rich heritage in the arts. The sources that we have used are noted in the chart, and additional material can be located in them. The Bibliography in this book may also be consulted for further help. Part of the teaching ministry of the church is to assist both young and old to become acquainted with the arts and the ways in which the arts may speak to us of the presence of God.

SOURCES

1. *Anthems for the Junior Choir,* Book 3. The Westminster Press, 1954.

2. *Familiar Hymns with Descants,* by Donald Kettring. The Westminster Press, 1956.

3. Oestreicher's Prints Inc.

4. *The Episcopal Hymnal* (1940), Hymn 466.

5. " Canticle of the Creatures " (No. 341), " Thanksgiving " (No. 365), " Conversion " (No. 758), in *Masterpieces of Religious Verse,* edited by James Dalton Morrison. Harper & Brothers, 1948.

6. *Christ and the Fine Arts,* by Cynthia Pearl Maus. Harper & Brothers, 1938.

7. International Art Publishing Company.

8. Artext Prints, Inc.

9. The Metropolitan Museum of Art.

10. *Anthems for the Mixed Choir.* The Westminster Press, 1948.

11. *Service Music for the Adult Choir.* The Westminster Press, 1956.

12. *Anthems for the Youth Choir,* Book 1. The Westminster Press, 1952.

13. *The Hymnbook,* Hymn 100.

II

"LOVE CAME DOWN
AT CHRISTMAS"

AT CHRISTMAS TIME OUR CHURCHES ARE FILLED WITH PEOPLE.
There are evergreen boughs at the windows, and many
candles light the sanctuary. Christmas is indeed a joyous
time and a time when there are many services. The services
of worship that comprise this section may be idea starters for
services that you can design. There are, however, several
things to keep in mind in creating your own services and
producing them.

Although Christmas is the festival of the birth of Christ,
the emphasis should not be only on the birth narrative. It is
good to capture the gentleness and mystery of the Nativity,
but this is not the most important message of Christmas. We
must also portray the grandeur of the incarnation of God in
Christ, and see beyond the manger to the cross and the salvation of the world. The Nativity may become so sweet that it
repulses us. We must instill in it the power and glory of a
God who acts in the world both at a historical point in time
and even today.

Christmas, more than any other time of year, is a time of
pageantry. If churches dip into the arts at all, it is most often
at Christmas, when a pageant is standard procedure. If this
is the case in your church, be sure that this once-a-year production is done well. Start months ahead to plan the pageant.

Have a conference with the choir director or the minister of music to plan the music that will be used. Think about the costumes. Bathrobed and turkish-toweled Wise Men have no place in the drama of the Christian church. Know your limitations and add a touch of excellence to what you do. It is only fitting that the reannouncement of the birth of Christ and his message to mankind be done with dignity.

" WE WOULD SEE JESUS "

This simple service of worship was created by boys and girls in grades four through six. It could be presented to other groups in the church school or to the entire congregation. If it is to be presented to the larger group, it could be augmented with additional anthems and could include a Christmas story or legend, either told by an adult or dramatized.

The service of worship should be presented in a darkened room. At the center should be the screen on which the slides will be projected. This screen could be framed with scrolled wood painted gold, or it could be wreathed with evergreens. Candelabra would afford a soft light, yet not detract from the projected slides. Spotlights can be used to highlight individuals as they speak. The speaking choir should be robed in order to direct attention away from their individual personalities, and they should memorize their parts. If the congregation is to participate in the service, careful consideration should be given as to when room lights are to be turned on and off.

The slides that are suggested are reproductions of some of the finest Christian art. If preparation is begun soon enough, the various scenes could be posed by members of the church school, and slides could be taken of the posed scenes and projected in place of the art reproductions. This can be very effective and is often more meaningful to the worshiping congregation.

Prelude: " O Come, O Come Emmanuel "

" Veni Emmanuel "

(During the prelude, the room lights go off and the picture Madonna and Child,[1] *by Murillo, is projected.)*

Narrator: For unto us a child is born, unto us a son is given: . . . and his name shall be called Wonderful, Counselor, The mighty God, The everlasting Father, The Prince of Peace.[2]

Hymn: " O Come, All Ye Faithful "   " Adeste fideles "

Prayer *(in unison, or by the speaking choir)*: Our Father, we ask forgiveness for our sins. Have mercy on us. Help us to see Jesus as our Savior, not as a warrior or a king. Help us to be good all our lives and to learn to love all people. Through Jesus Christ we pray. Amen.

Hymn: " O Little Town of Bethlehem "   " St. Louis "

(During the following Scripture and anthem, the picture The Adoration of the Shepherds,[1] *by Giorgione, is projected.)*

Narrator: And there were in the same country shepherds abiding in the field, keeping watch over their flock by night. And, lo, the angel of the Lord came upon them, and the glory of the Lord shone round about them; and they were sore afraid. And the angel said unto them,

Solo Voice: Fear not: for, behold, I bring you good tidings of great joy, which shall be to all people. For unto you is born this day in the city of David a Saviour, which is Christ the Lord. And this shall be a sign unto you; Ye shall find the babe wrapped in swaddling clothes, lying in a manger.

Narrator: And suddenly there was with the angel a multitude of the heavenly host praising God, and saying,

Speaking Choir:
>Glory to God in the highest,
>And on earth peace,
>Good will toward men.[3]

Anthem: "While Shepherds Watched "[4]   Williams

(*During the following Scripture, the picture* The Journey
of the Magi,[1] *by Sassetta, is projected.*)

Narrator: Now when Jesus was born in Bethlehem of Judea
in the days of Herod the king, behold, there came wise
men from the east to Jerusalem, saying,

Three Voices: Where is he that is born King of the Jews?
for we have seen his star in the east, and are come to
worship him.

Narrator: When Herod the king had heard these things, he
was troubled, and all Jerusalem with him. And when he
had gathered all the chief priests and scribes of the people
together, he demanded of them where Christ should be
born. And they said unto him,

Several Voices: In Bethlehem of Judea: for thus it is written
by the prophet. . . .

Narrator: Then Herod . . . privily called the wise men, inquired of them diligently what time the star appeared.
And he sent them to Bethlehem, and said,

Solo Voice: Go and search diligently for the young child;
and when ye have found him, bring me word again, that
I may come and worship him also.

Narrator: When they had heard the king, they departed;
and, lo, the star, which they saw in the east, went before
them, till it came and stood over where the young child

was. When they saw the star, they rejoiced with exceeding great joy. And when they were come into the house, they saw the young child with Mary his mother, and fell down, and worshipped him:

(*At this point, the picture* Adoration of the Magi,[1] *by Gentile de Fabriano, is projected*)

and when they had opened their treasures, they presented unto him gifts; gold, and frankincense, and myrrh. And being warned of God in a dream that they should not return to Herod, they departed into their own country another way.[5]

Speaking Choir:
> What can I give Him
> Poor as I am?

Voice 1:
> If I were a shepherd,
> I would give Him a lamb,

Voice 2:
> If I were a Wise Man,
> I would do my part, —

Voice 3:
> Yet what I can I give Him,

Speaking Choir:
> Give my heart.[6]

Prayer (*by the minister*): Our Heavenly Father, we thank you for the birth of Christ. We thank you for the angels who sang his birth to the shepherds. We thank you that there was a place where he could be born. We thank you for the star that guided the Wise Men. We thank you for all the people who through the years came to see Jesus. Through him we pray. Amen.

(*The speaking choir, divided into three groups, presents the following stanzas from different parts of the room, while the picture* Head of Christ,[1] *by Rembrandt, is projected.*)

Group 1:

We would see Jesus, lo! His star is shin-
ing
Above the stable while the angels sing;
There in a manger on the hay reclining,
Haste, let us lay our gifts before the
King.

Group 2:

We would see Jesus, on the mountain
teaching,
With all the listening people gathered
round;
While birds and flowers and sky above
are preaching
The blessedness which simple trust has
found.

Group 3:

We would see Jesus, in the early morn-
ing
Still as of old he calleth, " Follow me ";
Let us arise, all meaner service scorning,
Lord, we are thine, we give ourselves to
thee![7]

Hymn: " Joy to the World! "   " Antioch "

SOURCES

1. American Library Color Slide Company, Inc.
2. Isa. 9:6.
3. Luke 2: 8-14.
4. *Anthems for the Junior Choir,* Book 2. The Westminster Press, 1950.
5. Matt. 2:1-12.
6. Christina Rossetti.
7. J. Edgar Park from *New Worship and Song.* The Pilgrim Press.

"IN BETHL'EM TOWN"

This Christmas vesper service can be presented by older youth or adults. It combines several sources into a chancel drama that is effective when pantomimed while narrators or a speaking choir, or individuals taking speaking roles, present the thought. If a rhythmic choir interprets the various moods of the drama, the singing choir can introduce the theme during musical interludes or add musical settings within the drama. The service may be used as it is presented here for the Christmas program of the youth fellowship, following which the young people can carry some of the music of Christmas to others by going through the town singing carols. With the addition of other anthems from the church music library, the material can be enlarged and used for a candlelight service.

The chancel is an ideal place in which to present this service. Although the service is simple and should require only two complete rehearsals, it can be very effective if care is taken in the practicing of the several choirs, in the selection of costumes and properties, and in the use of lighting effects. This service is one of the many in this book which, though simple in presentation, may become a means for the expression of art forms in the program of the church.

Prelude: " The Night of the Star "[1]   Elmore
" Vom Himmel hoch, da komm' ich her "[2]
Arr. by Pachelbel

Hymn: " O Come, O Come, Emmanuel "
" Veni Emmanuel "

Speaking Choir: Let us now go even unto Bethlehem, and see this thing which is come to pass, which the Lord hath made known unto us.[3]

Anthem: " O Bethlehem " [4]   Arr. by Dickinson

A CHRISTMAS LITANY [5]

Minister: Thou whose thought did come to men on wings of radiant light, clothed in music that waked the hills to song,

Congregation: Receive anew the gifts of our worshiping.

Minister: Encompass us with mystery still.

Congregation: Conserve in our hearts all wonder.

Minister: As the shepherds in the Bethlehem fields were aroused by the glory which took possession of their night,

Congregation: Let us be stirred to perceive all things of highest good and follow till we find their source.

Minister: For all travelers this night we pray; for those who have the best rooms at the inn and for those who in their poverty have none,

Congregation: We ask thy blessing.

Minister: Remember all innkeepers of the world who graciously receive the late-arriving stranger.

Congregation: Give us the hospitality of generous hearts.

Minister: To those whose sorrow is accentuated by the gladness of this night,

Congregation: Let angels from the Holy Presence wing their way.

Minister: Lift our imagination to see a world wherein wisdom and love direct the action of its citizens.

All: Let us seek anew to bring our lives up to the level of God's purpose for the world. Amen.

Narrator: Centuries ago, God's purpose for the world was known but unheeded. Men lived for themselves and sought to find the purpose for the world within themselves. But God thought differently, and used the edict of a man to orient anew mankind.

Voice: And it came to pass in those days, that there went out a decree from Caesar Augustus, that all the world should be taxed. . . . And Joseph also went up from Galilee . . . unto the city of David, which is called Bethlehem, to be taxed with Mary his espoused wife.[6]

Organ: " Coventry Carol " [7]   Sixteenth century tune

(*Mary and Joseph proceed down center aisle, either speaking the words of " In the Town "* [8] *or pantomiming them as the narrator and soloists read them.*)

Narrator: But all people did not know as yet what was happening. Perhaps Joseph and Mary did not know the full answer that Christmas eve as their journey ended. They were thankful for a stable in which Mary might bear her child. She must have questioned somewhat — and Joseph even more: What child is this that we have given to the world?

(*The organ begins the playing of " Greensleeves." The rhythmic choir enters the chancel and moves in a graceful, yet diverse, rhythm so that it conveys a sense of seeking, of partial knowledge, and of anticipation. At the conclusion*

of the melody, the choir converges upon the innkeeper at
stage right and assumes a position that reflects despair as
the spotlight comes up on him.)

Unfortunately, the innkeeper did not know this unborn
child turned from his door.

Innkeeper:

> I am the keeper of the inn;
> What man will pity me?
> I heard one knocking at my gate
> And rose not up to see;
> I heard one crying in the dark
> In need and travail sore;
> I had no room to house God's Son,
> But turned him from my door.[9]

(*On the last line, the rhythmic choir moves in an attitude*
of expectancy as each lifts one arm toward the innkeeper
and the other arm outward toward the congregation. The
choir speaks the refrain.)

Rhythmic Choir:

> Goodman, rejoice! Nor grieve in vain.
> Tonight he seeks that door again![9]

(*After speaking, the choir moves in a seeking way to stage*
left, where it assumes a dejected position around the shep-
herds. During the movement, the narrator speaks.)

Narrator: For now came the shepherds, the light of the stars
still in their eyes and the song of the angels still ringing in
their ears. They came to worship a small baby in a manger.
Surely the townsfolk asked, "What do these shepherds
mean in worshiping this child?" Some of the shepherds
were not sure themselves, and there was one who did not
come.

Shepherd:

> Alas, I am that shepherdman
> Who watched the flocks by night
> And heard the tidings of good joy
> One brought on wings of light.
> But when the other shepherds ran
> To find in Bethlehem
> The child that was the Son of God,
> I would not go with them.[9]

(As the last line is spoken, the rhythmic choir moves as before and speaks the refrain.)

Rhythmic Choir:

> Good shepherd, cease; no more com-
>   plain.
> Tonight that child is born again![9]

(After speaking, the choir moves to stage center, where it awaits the coming of the Wise Men.)

Narrator: Wise men in the east also wondered as the stars moved across the sky. Some of them journeyed over the countryside to find a babe wrapped in swaddling clothes — a King in a manger. But there was one perhaps, or even two or more — we do not know — who stayed behind. He may have questioned and wished that he had come.

King:

> I am that king who stayed behind
> To keep a state forlorn:
> I let my wiser brothers seek
> The place where Christ was born.
> They bare him gold and frankincense
> As told in holy writ.
> I am the king who saw his star,
> Nor followed after it.[9]

(On the last line, the rhythmic choir moves as before and then speaks the refrain.)

Rhythmic Choir:
> Look up, poor king, and see for sign
> Tonight once more a star gives shine.[9]

Narrator: These found the answer — the innkeeper, the shepherds, and the Wise Men; and the long line of saints and martyrs, of common people and those of low degree who throughout the ages have sought to follow the way to the manger and the Holy Child. Not that they all knew at once, or in the same way, but ultimately they came to the realization that this Child was the Savior of the world.

(The rhythmic choir moves to the front of the chancel and speaks to the congregation.)

Rhythmic Choir:
> Good people, come! Receive Christ now,
> As here before him all men bow.

Anthem: " Ben Johnson's Carol "[10]   Sellew

Recessional Hymn:
> " O Come, All Ye Faithful "   " Adeste fideles "

Narrator: Let us pray.
> Lord Jesus, in the winter time,
> And to a world grown old in sin,
> Thou in thy loveliness did come,
> And as a child did enter in.
> The world was glad for thee and rang
> With carols herald angels sang.

Singing Choir:
> " O Come, All Ye Faithful " (Refrain only)
> " Adeste fideles "

Narrator: Let us with the Wise Men, lowly shepherds, and all the heavenly host praise and magnify thy holy name.

Singing Choir:
" Angels We Have Heard on High " (Refrain only)
" Gloria "

Benediction

Sources

1. Galaxy Music Corporation.

2. *Historical Organ Recitals,* Joseph Bonnet, ed., Vol. I. G. Schirmer, Inc.

3. Luke 2:15.

4. The H. W. Gray Company, Inc., No. 121.

5. " A Christmas Litany " has been arranged for this book from material by Abbie Graham.

6. Luke 2:1-5.

7. *The Oxford Book of Carols,* No. 22.

8. *Ibid.,* No. 91

9. " The Grieving Man," by Arthur Ketchum. Used by permission of *The Churchman.*

10. Schmitt, Hall & McCreary Company, No. 1641.

"WHY THE CHIMES RANG"

The story of "Why the Chimes Rang" has an appeal for young and old. It can be used effectively for a family service on Christmas Eve or as the basis for a service of gift-giving by the children of the church school. The story itself affords many opportunities for dramatization — as a chancel pageant, a pantomime, or a play. If there is not enough time to prepare the many costumes that are required and to rehearse the various parts, the story can stand alone if it is well narrated. Interspersing the spoken words of the story with Christmas hymns and anthems is very effective. Copies of "Why the Chimes Rang" can be secured from the Walter H. Baker Company, or a dramatization of the story can be secured from Samuel French, Inc.

As a chancel pageant, the first scene may be narrated by one or two readers, and the second scene, which takes place in the great cathedral, may be dramatized with as many characters as are desirable for the procession. In this procession, each person carries a suitable gift.

As the cathedral scene opens, the great organ is heard, and while the acolytes light the candles on the altar, the choir sings the two numbers by Britten. These anthems are in the style of the fifteenth century and are selected to create the medieval mood. Following this singing, the narrator continues the description of those attending the service, and as the various individuals present their gifts, the choir sings the suggested stanzas of "What Child Is This?," with the refrain, to the tune "Greensleeves." As each gift is presented to the minister, it is placed with appropriate dignity near the

34

altar. Since the narration is interspersed with singing during
the gift procession, careful timing is necessary. Prior to the
king's entrance, there is a fanfare of trumpets, followed by
stately and dignified music until the king reaches the altar, at
which time the choir sings the last stanza and the refrain of
" What Child Is This? " After the king has presented his gift
and the bells are not heard, a feeling of dejection and disap-
pointment is evident in the faces of the gift bearers. The organ continues its churchly strains in a subdued mood as the
little child comes forward unnoticed. Then is heard the
sound of bells high in the tower. For this, a carillon, hand-
bells, or recorded carillonic music may be used. As the bells
are heard, the participants kneel; they rise and remain in a
reverent mood when the choir sings the " Carol of the Bells."
Following this, the minister reads Matt. 25:34-40 and pro-
nounces the benediction. As the organist begins the recessional hymn, the gift bearers precede the choir down the
aisle.

The costuming for the pageant may be simple but should
make use of brilliant colors and rich fabrics. The gifts that
are presented should be large enough to be seen easily by all.
The Ceremony of Candlelighting, which precedes the pageant, can be as simple or elaborate as the local congregation
desires. It is often effective to have young boys or girls,
dressed as English waits, light the candles in the windows
and chancel. Their costumes would consist of red tights and
overblouses of the primary colors. A large, many-pointed collar and pointed shoes would complete the costume. If it is
desired, small bells could be attached to the shoes and collar
points. Music is sung by the choir during the candlelighting.

Prelude: " Noel "[1]   d'Aquin
              " Prelude (En Forme de Carillon) "[2]   Dubois

CEREMONY OF CANDLELIGHTING

Singing Choir:

"Masters in This Hall "[3]   Arr. by Holst
"No Candle Was There and No Fire "[4]   Lehmann
"Falan-tiding "[5]   Tyrolese carol

Hymn: " Hark! the Herald Angels Sing "   " Mendelssohn "

Call to Worship

Christmas Prayer

Anthems by the Junior Choir:

"Love Came Down at Christmas "[6]   Edward A. Mueller
"O Nightingale, Awake "[7]   Arr. by Dickinson
"Gentle Mary Laid Her Child "[8]

"Tempus Adest Floridum "

PAGEANT: "WHY THE CHIMES RANG"

Narration: Scene 1

Singing Choir: "Wolcum Yole "[9]   Britten
              "There Is No Rose "[10]   Britten

Narration: Scene 2, Introduction

Singing Choir:

"What Child Is This? " (Stanzas 1, 2)   "Greensleeves "

Narration: Scene 2

Singing Choir:

To him whose birth we celebrate
We bring our worldly treasure;
To God on high and Christ, his Son,
We give in fullest measure.[11]

(Courtiers and ladies of the court process down the aisle with gifts during the singing of the words above to the tune " Greensleeves.")

Narration: Scene 2, Writer, Musician, Artist Sequence

Singing Choir:
> In music sweet and most complete
> Our talents here we offer;
> A book for him, a painting too,
> And all to Christ we proffer.[11]

(The writer, musician, and artist process down the aisle as the words above are sung to " Greensleeves.")

Narration: Scene 2, Knight Sequence

Singing Choir:
> A knight am I, and warrior bold
> Whose sword is feared by all men;
> I lay it here, and do myself
> Most humbly pray for peace, then.[11]

(Knight proceeds down the aisle as the above words are sung.)

Narration: Scene 2, Queen Sequence

Singing Choir:
> My royal cloak as here displayed,
> An ermine stole, I tender;
> To Mary's Son, our blessed Lord,
> All love and praise I render.[11]

(The queen and her ladies in waiting process down the aisle as the above words are sung.)

Narration: Scene 2, King Sequence

Singing Choir:

"What Child Is This?" (Last stanza)   "Greensleeves"

(The king, followed closely by the jester, processes down the aisle.)

Narration: Scene 2, Conclusion

Bell Changes

Singing Choir: "Carol of the Bells" [12]   Wilhousky

Scripture: Matthew 25:34-40

Benediction

Recessional Hymn: "As with Gladness Men of Old" "Dix"

Sources

1. The St. Cecilia Series of Christmas Music, Set 2, compiled by John Holler. The H. W. Gray Company, Inc.

2. *Ten Pieces for the Organ,* arranged by Harker. Schirmer Library of Musical Classics, Vol. 1479. G. Schirmer, Inc.

3. *The Oxford Book of Carols,* No. 137.

4. Chappell & Co., Inc., No. 6020, SATB.

5. *The Oxford Book of Carols,* No. 121.

6. *Anthems for the Junior Choir,* Book 1. The Westminster Press, 1944.

7. Sacred Choruses, No. 179. The H. W. Gray Company, Inc.

8. *The Hymnbook,* Hymn 167.

9. Boosey & Hawkes, Inc., No. 1826.

10. *Ibid.,* No. 1827.

11. Original stanzas by W. Lawrence Curry and used by his permission.

12. Carl Fischer, Inc., No. 4604.

" EVERYWHERE, EVERYWHERE
CHRISTMAS TONIGHT "

Christmas is a time when families are together in the home and in the church. The Christian church must continually speak out to remind people everywhere of the true meaning of Christmas, and family Christmas celebrations are a part of the witness of the church at this season. The following dramatization was first produced at a church family night at the beginning of Advent. It reminds Christians the world over of their unity in Christ and attempts to attach Christian meaning to some of the symbols of Christmas. It also tries to capture the love and closeness that members of the family feel for one another. The closing tableau may remind families the world over that Christ can come and be a part of their Christmas, just as he came into his own family many years ago.

Prior to the dramatization, families may gather in the church social hall or dining room to sing familiar carols. If the service is to be held early in Advent, gifts may be brought and placed on a large, undecorated Christmas tree. The giving of these gifts can be planned for in Sunday church school classes. They may, for example, be sent to a mission school in which the local church has an interest. Table and room decorations can be planned by the youth groups of the church. Christmas cookies and punch are often served on such occasions, but since it is hoped that the message of the dramatization will be carried immediately to the homes represented, it is suggested that the group be dismissed following the dramatization. If a closing service of worship is desired, it should be led by a family, with the parents and children taking part in the service. Encouragement could be given to the other families of the church to re-enact this time of devotion in their own homes.

Instrumental Music:
" Deck the Halls with Boughs of Holly " English carol

(*The curtains begin to open as the carol ends. The stage is relatively bare. There is a partially decorated Christmas tree, large enough so that a stepladder is needed to reach the top, at stage left. Grouped around the tree are members of an American family. The father is on the stepladder and is almost ready to put the star on the top of the tree. With him is a small child. Another child kneels at the base of the tree, putting the finishing touches on the crèche. The mother is stringing cranberries and popcorn for the tree, and another child is adding ornaments. The characters stand as if frozen until the music stops; then they begin their action. The time is Christmas Eve.*)

Child 1: Bright Christmas balls to remind me of the jewels in the crowns of the Wise Men.

Father: And the star on the top of the tree, high up, and bright, to remind us of the star God sent to guide the Wise Men to the stable in Bethlehem.

Mother: Let's not forget the everyday things — like my popcorn and cranberries. Even though they are ordinary, they add a festive touch to the tree. They can remind us of God's goodness to us in giving us food for our bodies. And even before we decorated our trees with colored lights and glass balls, our grandmothers and grandfathers used garlands of cranberries and popcorn and ever so many candles.

Child 2: But now we have electric lights. I'll bet the children who lived a hundred years ago would like to see our tree with all the electric lights. They really missed a lot.

Father: Perhaps they did, but perhaps Christmas meant more to them.

Child 3: Why? Christmas means lots to me, with all the presents.

Mother: I think that's what Daddy means. Perhaps we think too much of the presents we give and receive. That's why we try to remember part of the Christmas story when we decorate the tree.

Child 2: That's why we have the manger scene underneath the tree — so that we won't forget the birth of Christ.

Father: Yes, the manger scene is the one thing that reminds us of Christmas.

Child 3: Doesn't everyone have a Christmas tree?

Father: I'm afraid not. At least not a Christmas tree like ours. In some lands Christmas trees don't grow. Children in the warm equatorial lands would have to use a palm tree if they wanted a Christmas tree!

Child 1: Like the palm tree in our manger scene?

Mother: That's right. Perhaps a palm tree might make a better Christmas tree than our pine tree does. It might remind us more of the land where Jesus was born.

Father: But there are some children who don't even have a palm tree for a Christmas tree. Just the same, they can remember Christmas. They may not have a lot of gifts either, but Christmas means much to them.

Child 2: They can think — they can think about Jesus.

Father: The story of the birth of Jesus is the one thing that reminds everyone of Christmas.

Mother: All around the world, where it's hot and where it's very cold, families are hearing the story of Jesus.

Child 3: Do they all hear the same story?

Mother: The same story, told in different languages. All around the world it's Christmas tonight, and boys and girls are hearing the same story that I tell you each Christmas Eve. Let's sing a carol, and then we'll hear the Christmas story.

Instrumental Music:
" Silent Night! Holy Night! "   " Stille Nacht "

(*As the music begins, the curtains close. Four families take their places on graduated tiers. There is a family from Africa, one from Sweden, one from Japan, and one from an island in the Pacific. Behind the tiers is a stylized Gothic window. The upper part is painted to suggest stained glass. The lower sections are open and reveal a starry sky. The tableau figures are framed in the lower portions of the window. As the curtains open, the lights dim. There is a spotlight on the narrating family gathered around the mother, who is seated in a chair.*)

Mother: All around the world, families are gathered together to hear the Christmas story. In a small house in the hot jungle of Africa, a mother tells the story to her children. A father in Japan tells his family about the wonderful story of Jesus' birth. In Sweden, a sheaf of grain has been fastened to a pole for the birds, and the family has gath-

ered to hear the good news which the angels brought to
the shepherds. On the beach of an island in the Pacific, a
family watches the stars and thinks about the star that
guided the Wise Men to the stable. " Everywhere, everywhere, Christmas tonight! "

Swedish Family:
>Christmas in lands of the fir tree and
>   pine,

Island Family:
>Christmas in lands of the palm tree and
>   vine,

Japanese Family:
>Christmas where snow peaks stand sol-
>   emn and white,

African Family:
>Christmas where cornfields stand sunny
>   and bright,

All:
>Everywhere, everywhere, Christmas to-
>   night!

Mother:
>For the Christ-Child who comes is the
>   Master of all,
>No palace too great and no cottage too
>   small;
>The angels who welcome him sing
>   from the height,
>" In the City of David, a King in his
>   might."

All:
> Everywhere, everywhere, Christmas to-
> night!
> Then let every heart keep its Christmas
> within,

Japanese:
> Christ's pity for sorrow,

African:
> Christ's hatred for sin,

Islander:
> Christ's care for the weakest,

Swedish:
> Christ's courage for right,

African:
> Christ's dread of the darkness,

Swedish:
> Christ's love of the light,

All:
> Everywhere, everywhere, Christmas to-
> night! [1]

Mother: All the world looks toward Bethlehem on Christmas night. Across the centuries we take our minds and
hearts, and hear again the wonderful story. Many years
ago, when Caesar Augustus was emperor, it became necessary to count all the people in his empire. This included
the land of Palestine. Every family in the land had to go
to the place from which the head of the family had come
to have its name recorded. Joseph of Nazareth, a car-
penter, and his wife, Mary, made the long journey to
Bethlehem,

(Mary and Joseph appear in the window)

because Joseph's family was the family of King David, and Bethlehem was his home city. Mary was soon to become a mother, and while Mary and Joseph were in Bethlehem, the time came for the baby to be born. There was no room in the inn, so the baby was born in a stable.

(Shepherds appear in the window)

There were some shepherds in that neighborhood, keeping watch through the night over their flock in the open fields. Suddenly a bright light shone in the sky, and an angel appeared to them.

(Angel joins the shepherd group in the window)

The angel said, " Do not be frightened, for I bring you good news of a great joy which is to be felt by all people. This night in Bethlehem a baby was born. He is your Savior and Lord. If you will go to Bethlehem, you will find the child wrapped up in swaddling cloths and lying in a manger." And suddenly there appeared with the angel a great number of the heavenly host, praising God and saying, " Glory to God in the highest, and on earth peace, good will to men."

(Shepherds and angels exit)

When the angels left them and returned to heaven, the shepherds hurried to Bethlehem and found Mary and Joseph and the child.

(Nativity grouping in the window)

The shepherds told everyone what the angel had said to them. Everyone who heard it was amazed at what the shepherds told them, but Mary treasured up all they had said and thought about it later on. The shepherds went back to their fields, singing praises to God for all they had seen and heard.

(*Wise Men appear in the window*)

Before the shepherds made their journey to Bethlehem, other men were getting ready for a journey. To the east of the village of Bethlehem, three Wise Men had seen a new star in the sky, and set out to follow where it led. They traveled across deserts and over mountains. They went through big cities and small villages. At last they came to the city of Jerusalem and to the palace of King Herod. They thought a new king had been born in the palace, and they told the king that they had come to worship this new prince. Herod knew nothing about this, so he called all his advisers together. They told him that a new king was to be born in Bethlehem, so it was to Bethlehem that the Wise Men went. There they came to the stable, and saw Mary, Joseph, and the baby. The kings from the east went in and worshiped the child, giving to him gifts of gold, frankincense, and myrrh. King Herod had asked them to come back to him and tell him about the child, but an angel appeared to the Wise Men in a dream, and told them to go home another way. And that is the story that is told around the world, the story that never grows old, the wonderful story of the birth of Jesus so many years ago. Now it's time for bed. Let's sing "Away in a Manger" and think of the birth of Jesus as it is told around the world, for everywhere, everywhere, there is Christmas tonight.

(*The lights go down until the figures are seen in shadowy outline. The fathers in the groups stand, and each mother*

*picks up one of the little children. In the window, Mary is
seen holding the baby while Joseph stands beside her. All
sing " Away in a Manger." The curtain falls.*)

SOURCES

1. Phillips Brooks, " Christmas Everywhere."

A ROUND OF CAROLS

In the day and age in which we live, we often forget
the true meaning of Christmas. The family service that follows is designed to usher in the Christmas season in a Christian context. It should be presented near the beginning of
Advent, with each family present receiving suggestions for
a ceremony of the Advent wreath.[1] The service is designed
in four parts: the Wassail Hour, during which time various
musical groups present traditional carols; the Dinner; the
Carol Service; and the Service of Worship, based on the
Ceremony of the Advent Wreath.

The entire service centers around one of the church families, designated as the Host's Family. This family, in period
dress, greets the guests, sits at a special table in the dining
room, where pages in Old English costumes serve, and leads
the service of worship.

PART I

Here we come a-wassailing
Among the leaves so green.[2]

(As the guests arrive, they are greeted by the host and his
family. Hostesses, dressed in ball gowns, preside at the
wassail bowls. The tables are covered with white linen and
are graced with holly and ivy and silver candlesticks. Several musical groups alternate in providing music. If possible, an English recorder group and a string ensemble
should be among these groups. When the guests have been
together for a time, the lights dim. A town crier, preceded

*by his servant ringing a bell, appears and reads the procla-
mation.*)

Crier: Forasmuch as it hath pleased Almighty God to bring
us to this Advent season in the year of our Lord One
Thousand, Nine Hundred, and Sixty _____, and since
we have come to this season blessed with good health, happiness, and an abundance of material goods, it is fitting
that we should come together in this community of faith,
giving thanks for all that we have received and extending
to one another the good will which abounds among us.
We therefore proclaim this night as the beginning of the
Christmas season, and exhort those who are gathered here
to keep this season of Advent and Christmas in the true
spirit of Christ, giving thanks, deepening our faith, and
striving to live lives worthy of the One whose advent and
birthday we celebrate at this time, even Jesus Christ our
Lord.

PART II

The boar's head in hand bear I,
Bedecked with bays and rosemary.[3]

Host: Let us now pause to ask God's blessing upon us and
to give thanks.

Minister: Prayer of Invocation and Thanksgiving

Host: From olden times, the Christmas season has been one
of feasting as families gather around the table. As a church
family, we gather this night for food and fellowship. As
the food is carried into the dining room, we shall hear a
carol that is associated with the Christmas feast at Queen's
College, Oxford. The legend behind this carol tells of an
Oxford student who, when walking in the forest, was sud-

denly confronted with a wild boar. Having no weapons with him, he shoved his Greek grammar into the mouth of the boar, causing him to choke. He then triumphantly brought the boar back to his college, where it was served with much merriment. Let us now repair to the dining room to hear this carol and join one another around the tables.

Solo and Choir: " The Boar's Head Carol " [4]

Old English carol

(*During the singing of the carol, costumed pages carry the boar's head and other dishes to the host's table.*)

PART III

What sweeter music can we bring
Than a carol, for to sing
The birth of this our heavenly King? [5]

Host: Our Christmas music has come to us from many lands and many peoples. Music is the thread that binds us together with the past and unites us with all parts of the world. One of the earliest announcements in song of the birth of Christ was in the Latin of the Roman Catholic Church. In the distance we hear the announcement, " Hodie Christus natus est ": Today Christ is born. Following this solo, the choirs will process to the hymn " O Come, All Ye Faithful." The members of the congregation are asked to join with the choirs after the first stanza has been sung in Latin.

Solo: " Hodie Christus Natus Est " [6]   Britten

Choirs: " Adeste, fideles "   "Adeste fideles"
  Adeste, fideles,
  Laeti triumphantes;

Venite, venite in Bethlehem;
Natum videte regem angelorum.
Venite, adoremus Dominum.

Congregation: " O Come, All Ye Faithful "
" Adeste fideles "

Host: Caroling has become a lovely English tradition and is still carried on today. Groups of carolers, called " waits," go from house to house on Christmas Eve singing the familiar carols. While we are not sure of the exact meaning of the word " wait," some people think that it comes from the idea of waiting for the news of the angels. Christmas in England is a time of merrymaking and good cheer. The holly and the ivy decorate the homes for the season, and the bringing in of the Yule log is an important ceremony. In old England, December 26, St. Stephen's Day, was set aside as Boxing Day. On this day it was customary for the poor to receive money from the rich. A Christmas box was carried to receive these gifts. Today in England, servants often receive boxes of fruit or sweets on St. Stephen's Day. According to legend, good King Wenceslas had compassion on the poor on St. Stephen's Day. The narrative of this old legend is contained in this English carol.

Choir: " Good King Wenceslas "   " Tempus adest floridum "

Host: An English carol that we all know and enjoy singing is " The First Nowell." Let us join together in singing the first stanza.

Congregation: " The First Nowell "   " The First Nowell "

Hostess: In France, the Nativity scene, or " crèche," is of great importance at Christmas. In the French home, candles are lighted before the crèche on Christmas Eve and kept burning until Epiphany, January 6. In French homes also, we will find Christmas hoops, made from foliage, apples, nuts, and colored eggshells. Christmas cookies are baked in the shape of the infant Christ-child and it is not uncommon to hear French children speak of eating the infant Jesus. Caroling is also a French custom. French carols are known as "noels." One of the lovely French noels is "Angels We Have Heard on High." The refrain to this carol is the Latin "Gloria in Excelsis Deo" and recalls to us the times when carols were sung in Latin.

Choir: "Angels We Have Heard on High"   "Gloria"

Host: There are many quaint and beautiful customs connected with Christmas in Poland. Hay or straw is placed under the tablecloth at the Christmas feast, and in many homes a chair is provided at the table for the Holy Child. Some children believe that the Good Stars bring them their Christmas trees. Mother Star is a beautiful woman dressed in white robes. Father Star gives gifts to those children who say their prayers and sing hymns correctly. From Poland comes the lovely carol "Infant Holy." It tells us the story of the Nativity in simple language.

Choir: "Infant Holy" [7]   Polish carol

Host: If we were having a Christmas dinner in Russia, we would find straw under the tablecloth to remind us of the manger in Bethlehem. The Russian children believe Babushka is the giver of gifts. There is a legend that tells that Babushka misdirected the Wise Men when they were on their way to see the Christ-child, and that when the holy family came to her to find shelter on the way to Egypt, she refused them. When she learned of her mistake, she set out at once to find the Christ-child. Now, on Christmas

Eve, people believe that she journeys through the land and enters the homes to see if the Christ-child lives there. After she looks at the sleeping children, she slips a toy under each pillow and then goes on to continue her search for the Christ. From Russia comes this beautiful carol of the angels.

Choir: " The Angels' Song " [8]   Russian carol

Hostess: The Christmas tree that is in most of our homes at this season was originated in Germany. It is said that Martin Luther, attempting to describe the beauty of the stars at night to his wife and children, went out into the garden, cut a small fir tree, and put some lighted candles on its branches to represent stars. In other parts of Germany, trees were decorated with colored paper, apples, and foil. From Germany comes this carol that tells us about the Christmas tree.

Choir: " O Tannenbaum "   German folk song

Host: Another lovely German carol that is a favorite of children and adults alike is " Good Christian Men, Rejoice." Let us sing together the stanzas of this well-known carol.

Congregation: " Good Christian Men, Rejoice "
                                " In dulci jubilo "

Hostess: In Czechoslovakia, carolers go from house to house carrying the crèche. It was traditional at one time for some of the younger boys to dress as the Three Kings during the caroling. The children in Czechoslovakia look to St. Nicholas to bring their gifts. December 6 is the day that is celebrated in his honor. The Czechoslovakian children believe that St. Nicholas descends to earth on a golden cord. Angels guide him through the countryside and bring gifts to the children. From Bohemia, a part of Czechoslovakia, comes our next carol.

Choir: " Angels and Shepherds " [9]   " Kommet, ihr Hirten "

Host: From Mexico comes the custom of the *posada*. *Posada* means sheltering place and reminds us of the search for lodging by Mary and Joseph. Many families join together in a *posada*. Some carry statues of Mary, Joseph, and the angels, and all carry lighted candles. There is a great deal of singing as these people walk through the streets. When they come to the house of a friend, they stop and ask for lodging. At first the request is denied, but after a time, all are welcomed into the house, and after a prayer before the crèche, there are refreshments and dancing. Let us now listen to the Mexican carol that tells us about this custom.

Choir: " Let the Doors Fly Open Wide " [10]
Mexican folk song

Hostess: The carols that we sing in this country are most often borrowed from other lands and people. There are some Negro carols that are American in origin. The music of these carols, like many of the spirituals, is syncopated in rhythm. We hear now the Negro carol " Rise Up, Shepherd, an' Foller."

Choir: " Rise Up, Shepherd, an' Foller " [11]
American spiritual

Host: Another carol that was written by an American is " It Came Upon the Midnight Clear." Let us join in singing the first stanza of this carol.

Congregation: " It Came Upon the Midnight Clear "
" Carol "

Host: Christmas, as we have learned from hearing some of these customs, is celebrated in many ways and at different times. Christmas is not just a day but a season of the year when we think of gaiety and good times. Traditionally, Christmas in England is celebrated for twelve days. One of the gay carols that incorporates this idea is " The Twelve Days of Christmas." The choirs will now sing this joyful carol.

Choirs: " The Twelve Days of Christmas " [12]

Traditional carol

PART IV

Let every house be ready tonight,
The children gathered, the candles alight,
That music to hear, to see that sight. [13]

Host: Christmas is indeed a joyous time, but in the midst of all the merriment we must not forget the true meaning of this season. We hope that all of you will take this as your creed during this Christmas season.

As time runs out each year
We celebrate
The Advent of our Christ.
God hopes this year,
As he has in all the years gone by,
To have Christ born in you:
Prepare your heart for him.

Hostess: One of the ways in which our church family can prepare for the coming of Christ anew is by participating in the Ceremony of the Advent Wreath. Holding family services during the four weeks of Advent is an ancient custom that comes to us from the countries of Europe. During these weeks, preparations for Christmas are made, the house is decorated, and the spirit of Christmas permeates the air. It is also a time for families to strengthen their spiritual bonds and for them to prepare for the coming of the Christ-child. To this end, family services are held one evening each week for the four weeks before Christmas. From one of our European neighbors comes the Ceremony of the Advent Wreath. It is customary to light the first candle during the first family service, the first and second during the second service, and so on. We hope that you will begin this custom in your homes this year. Join with us as we hear the Christmas story and light the first Advent candle.

Child: Luke 2:8-20

Congregation: " O Little Town of Bethlehem " " St. Louis "

(First candle is lighted.)

Child: Let us pray. May our hearts be ready, O God, for the season ahead and for the birth of Jesus. May we ever be watching and faithful. Through Jesus Christ our Lord. Amen.

Benediction

SOURCES

1. See Christina Hole, *Christmas and Its Customs* (M. Barrows and Company, Inc., 1958), Ch. 2, p. 14, for information about the preparation of the wreath.

2. *The Oxford Book of Carols,* No. 15.

3. *Ibid.,* No. 19.

4. *Ibid.*

5. *Ibid.,* No. 122.

6. *A Ceremony of Carols,* by Benjamin Britten. Boosey & Hawkes, Inc.

7. *Anthems for the Junior Choir,* Book 4. The Westminster Press, 1959.

8. *Anthems for the Junior Choir,* Book 2.

9. *Christmas: Its Carols, Customs and Legends,* compiled and arranged by Ruth Heller. Schmitt, Hall & McCreary Company, 1948.

10. *The Whole World Singing,* compiled by Edith Lovell Thomas. Friendship Press, 1950.

11. Heller, *op. cit.*

12. Arr. by Frederic Austin. Novello & Co., Ltd. (The H. W. Gray Company, Inc.).

13. *The Oxford Book of Carols,* No. 191.

FAMILIES AROUND THE WORLD

Many churches today are helping parents and children prepare themselves spiritually for Christmas through family services of worship, the teaching of new carols and old Christmas hymns, and the telling of legends and stories. Americans have inherited Christmas customs and traditions from various countries, and it is interesting at this time of year to know how other Christian families prepare for Christmas. The celebration of the birth of Christ is a wonderful way to unite ideas from all over the world and thus to witness to our unity in the Child of Bethlehem.

The following service is approximately an hour in length and may serve as a guide after which to pattern other services using music, art, and legends of other countries not included in this program. This type of program is best used on Sunday afternoon or in the early evening for a church-wide family service. Old and young alike can take part and join with the congregation in the true spirit of Christian sharing.

To organize a service such as this in the busyness of the Christmas season, the director should choose one person who will be responsible for each episode. It will be this person's duty to schedule rehearsal time, secure costumes and properties, and arrange the stage setting. These sub-rehearsals may be short so that persons in the various episodes will not have to wait for hours to rehearse. One complete rehearsal is all that is necessary.

Following the program, food characteristic of one of the countries may be served. The persons in the performance may remain in costume and help in the serving, thereby making the social hour colorful and providing an interesting topic for conversation.

The description under each episode includes suggestions for the setting. After you have read these descriptions, we suggest that stage diagrams be made. There are slight changes in furniture and properties for each episode and the person in charge of each episode can prepare the properties indicated. The stage may be set while the choir is singing the intervening selection. The setting of the stage may be speeded up if each participant is responsible for one or two properties in his episode.

Prelude: Fantasia on three Christmas carols. (*The organist may improvise on " As with Gladness Men of Old," " It Came Upon the Midnight Clear," and " Love Came Down at Christmas."*)
> " Choral Prelude on ' In dulci jubilo ' " [1]
> Bach-Dickinson

PROLOGUE

Hymn: " As with Gladness Men of Old "   " Dix "

Choir: " Let Our Gladness Know No End " [2]
> Old Bohemian melody

Hymn: " It Came Upon the Midnight Clear "   " Carol "

Reading: " The Gift of Love "
> I am the spirit of true Christmas love,
> Bringing you gladness and joy;
> Spreading the light from the heavens
>   above;
> Shining on each Christmas tree.
> I am the spirit behind every gift

That loved ones bring gladly to you.
I am the hope giving mankind the lift
And brightening the world with cheer.
I am the knowledge that comes from
above,
Guiding your thoughts to the crib;
I am the message that's known as God's
love.
With peace and good will, follow me.

Hymn: " Love Came Down at Christmas " " Hermitage "

EPISODE I

(The scene is the interior of an American home. There is a large kitchen with a center fireplace. Father is seated at a table, putting Christmas seals on family packages and cards. Mother and two or three girls are grouped around a large table, decorating Christmas cookies. One child is tying up greens with a bright red ribbon. A junior age boy is trying on his choir robe for his mother to check. An older girl is wrapping gifts for an old people's home. Two small children are trimming the Christmas tree, which is near the fireplace. The narrator begins as the curtain opens.)

Narrator: Christmas in America is not like Christmas in any other land, for it is like Christmas in many lands. As children of other countries became children of America, they brought with them to their churches and homes in a new country rich treasures of custom and tradition. And into the pattern that is now America's Christmas have been woven colorful threads of bits of Christmas from everywhere.

Carols from England, Saint Lucia celebrations from Sweden, the Christmas tree from Germany, the Yule log from England and France, the Christmas crib from Poland, the birds' Christmas from Norway — these, and many more delightful customs, are now a part of Christmas in America.

The first Christmas in America was celebrated in Jamestown in 1607. In Plymouth, Christmas for the Puritans was a day of solemn worship. Persons who were found to be boisterous or irreverent were fined five shillings. Bells have been played and carols have been sung on Beacon Hill in Boston from the time of the early settlers, and this custom is duplicated in many parts of our country. Interesting legends have sprung up in various areas of our country, such as the old plantation legend in the South that all beasts lean toward the star of Bethlehem on Christmas Eve.

In the typical American home we find the following activities on Christmas Eve: Christmas seals are put on family packages; cookies are decorated for baskets for the needy; greens are wrapped for the sick; a choir robe is fixed for the candlelight service in the church; the small children trim the Christmas tree; gifts are wrapped for an old people's home; the family worship is based upon the Family Preparation Service for Christmas that the church school has suggested.

Surrounded as we are by the commercial aspects of Christmas, we are likely to forget that we are celebrating the birth of Jesus. In this Christian home, true love at Christmas is being expressed through the family's preparation.

(*During this narration, the curtains have opened to reveal the American family taking part in the various Christmas*

*preparations that the narrator has mentioned. The curtains
close during the anthem.*)

Anthem: " The Angels Sang a Gloria " [3]   Curry

Hymn: " O Little Town of Bethlehem "   " St. Louis "

EPISODE II

(*The setting is the same, but additional properties, described in the narration that follows, have been added.*)

Narrator: The burning of the yule log to celebrate Christmas
is a tradition in the English household. On Christmas Eve
the log is cut and hauled to the house with great ceremony. According to legend, a piece chopped off and saved
for the following year brings good luck. Each year the
yule log is lighted by the piece reserved from the year before, and is kept glowing for twelve days.
On the table we see the boar's head, the plum pudding,
and the mince pie, traditional on the English table at
Christmas time. The holly and the ivy are placed in the
windows and on the mantlepiece, indicating that the
Christ-child has entered this home. The holly symbolizes
the crown of thorns, and the red berries, the blood of
Christ. The ivy's heart-shaped leaves are in the shape of
the footprint of God.

(*The choir sings as the curtains close.*)

Anthems: " The Boar's Head Carol " [4]   Old English carol
          " I Saw Three Ships " [5] Traditional English tune

EPISODE III

(*As the curtain opens on the French scene, small children
are preparing the crèche and placing candles before it. The*

*mother is preparing a basket of food for the Feast of the
Christ-Child. On a table are the bird costumes that the
mother will need to dress the children for the " Carol of
the Birds.")*

Narrator: The crèche is of great importance in France.
Lighted candles are placed before it in the home and they
burn until Epiphany. People go through the streets singing noels and collecting pennies thrown to them for the
poor.
The midnight mass will be attended by the family. Following this, the family will enjoy food which they have
brought to the church. Tradition says that they are guests
of the Holy Family. You see the mother preparing a basket
of food to take to the church. Neighboring children have
joined members of this family for a rehearsal of the " Carol
of the Birds." The French people honor birds, beasts, and
all of nature at this time.
On Twelfth-night there is a Feast of the Kings, a ceremony celebrating the arrival of the Magi. At this ceremony
we see family reunions, gift-giving, and feasting.

Anthem: " Carol of the Birds " [6]   Bas-Quercy carol

*(While this carol is sung, four or five children, dressed as
birds, move in rhythm to the music.)*

Hymn: " Hearken, All! What Holy Singing " or
        " Angels We Have Heard on High "   " Gloria "
                                    (French carol tune)

(At the beginning of the hymn, the curtains close.)

EPISODE IV

*(In place of the kitchen table, there is a long, narrow desk
or table on which stands a music rack and a keyboard, giv-*

*ing the impression of an organ. A bench is placed in front
of the table.*)

Narrator: The scene of the German family takes place in the
home of Martin Luther. We find Luther at the organ
(*curtains open*), accompanying one of his daughters in a
lovely Christmas carol. The tree will be trimmed with
stars with Scripture verses on them. A Christmas wreath is
hung in the window on the first Sunday in Advent and a
candle added each Sunday until Christmas.

The Christmas tree, the evergreen, is a symbol of Christ,
the Tree of everlasting life. A tradition among the Ger-
mans says that the pine tree concealed Joseph and Mary
from the soldiers of Herod on their flight into Egypt.

(*The curtains close as the choir sings the following numbers.*)

Anthems: " Ah, Dearest Jesus, Holy Child " [7]
                                    " Von Himmel hoch "
          " O Tannenbaum "   German folk song

EPISODE V

(*Before the curtain opens, the " organ " is removed, and
chairs are placed around a large kitchen table, where
father, mother, and children are seated. In the center of
the table is a straw-filled manger. A small doll in swaddling clothes is placed in the manger by the father. On a
side table are placed rush lanterns. The narrator reads as
the curtain opens.*)

Narrator: Christmas in the Italian home is a deeply religious
experience. The *presepio,* or crib, characterizes Christmas
in Italy. For twenty-four hours preceding Christmas Eve,
fasting is observed and a religious atmosphere prevails.

The family gather around the evening table and pass the Christ-child doll from person to person. "Christ is with us," they say. The doll is placed in the manger by the father, and following this, they prepare to go to mass. Each person carries his rush lantern to light his way to the cathedral.

The shepherds come down from the mountains, playing bagpipes. They stop at the doors and wish all the joys of Christmas to everyone. A wooden spoon is left at each door to mark the place where they will return to sing carols. The carol "In Bethlehem" is a traditional Italian melody that Handel used for the theme of his pastoral symphony in *The Messiah*. The carol "Falan-tiding," which likewise the choir will sing, comes from the highlands of the Italian Tyrol, and sparkles with the light gaiety so typical of those people.

Anthems: "In Bethlehem" [8]   Old Italian carol
      "Falan-tiding" [9]   Tyrolian carol tune

(*The family leave the scene, each person carrying his lantern.*)

EPISODE VI

(*The curtain opens on the scene of a Swedish kitchen. On the large table is a white cloth and a coffee service on a tray. Lucia, with her crown of lighted candles, pours coffee as her brothers and sisters enter. On a table at one side of the stage are dunce caps, star sticks, and candles.*)

Narrator: The Festival of Santa Lucia is celebrated in Sweden on December 13 and commemorates the Italian maiden, known for beauty, generosity, warmth, and courage, who died a martyr's death centuries ago. She is depicted as a maiden wearing a crown of lighted candles as she goes about the village gathering alms for the poor. Other maidens, wearing green garlands, attend her, and she is accompanied by Star Boys, who represent the servants of the Wise Men. Little elves who dwell among the Christmas greens scamper beside them.

The festival begins early in each home when the eldest daughter, dressed as Lucia, brings coffee and buns to her parents. As the day progresses, she and other members of the family re-enact the Lucia legend as they process through the town.

(*As the choir begins to sing, the procession, with Lucia as its head, leaves the stage and proceeds down the center aisle. Following the epilogue, they greet the guests at the coffee hour, which is traditional at the festival.*)

Anthem: " Santa Lucia " [10]   Neapolitan boat song

Santa Lucia,
Thy light is glowing,
Through darkest winter night
Comfort bestowing.
Dreams float on wings bedight,
Comes then the morning light,
Santa Lucia!
Santa Lucia!

Through silent winter gloom,
Thy song comes winging
To waken earth anew
Glad carols bringing.
Come, thou, O Queen of Light,
Wearing thy crown so bright.
Santa Lucia!
Santa Lucia!

Santa Lucia,
Christmas foretelling,
Fill hearts with hope and cheer,
Dark fears dispelling.
Bring to the world again
Peace, and good will to men.
Santa Lucia!
Santa Lucia!

EPILOGUE

Anthem: " In the Bleak Mid-Winter " [11]   Lundquist

Christmas Prayer

Choral Response

SOURCES

1. Historical Recital Series, No. 30. The H. W. Gray Company, Inc.

2. *Anthems for the Mixed Choir.*

3. Church Music Review, No. 1602. The H. W. Gray Company, Inc.

4. *The Oxford Book of Carols,* No. 19.

5. *Ibid.,* No. 18.

6. Heller, *Christmas: Its Carols, Customs and Legends,* p. 84.

7. *The Methodist Hymnal,* Hymn 108; *The Hymnbook,* Hymn 158.

8. Heller, *op. cit.,* p. 71.

9. *The Oxford Book of Carols,* No. 121.

10. From *Christmastime in Sweden: The Christmas Festival,* by Alice J. Sorensen, p. 12. Copyright, 1955, by Augustana Book Concern. Used by permission.

11. Summy-Birchard Publishing Company, No. 1492, SATB.

" THE MIRACLE OF THE MANGER "

The following pageant was written to present the traditional Christmas story in a contemporary setting. It was so designed that it will appeal by text to the adults of the congregation and by visual image to the children. It is very effective if it is presented as a vesper service in the chancel. Since lighting is so important to the service, it is imperative that the room can be effectively darkened.

The major portion of the pageant is carried by three narrators, assisted by a speaking choir, a singing choir, a rhythmic choir, and soloists. The narrators and the speaking choir are at one side of the chancel. The singing choir is in the balcony. At one side of the chancel are platforms of various heights. The highest platform is to represent the stable at Bethlehem. For the final tableau, the participants are grouped on the various levels, with hands joined one to the other. The rhythmic choir occupies the chancel floor, extending down the chancel steps into the center aisle. The last person holds her arm outstretched to the congregation, indicating that they are part of the worshiping throng.

Authentic costuming is essential to the production, and care should be taken to assure a pleasing arrangement of color and position during the last tableau. The rhythmic choir may be costumed in the native dress of several countries, or they may be gowned in red, black, brown, white, and yellow to represent the races of the world.

Prelude: Improvisation on Advent hymns [1]

(*The commotion of a crowd outside the church is heard. The bell of the street-corner Santa rings incessantly. There*

*is amplified music, so that all the world may hear. The
speaking choir enters from the rear of the church and
walks down the center aisle. Some carry large packages;
others, smaller bundles; one or two are reading the news-
paper. All are dressed in outdoor attire.)*

Voice 1:

> The bargains at the big store
> In the center of town
> Are too good to pass up.
> The evening paper is getting
> Heavier by the day
> With all the attractive
> Advertising that tempts us
> To buy just one more gift.

Voice 2:

> We shopped for the big things
> Weeks ago
> So we wouldn't be disappointed.
> But there are still some gifts
> To be picked up:
> The small toys for the children's stock-
>   ings,
> Which we can get in the dime store —
> The kind that will be broken
> Before the day is half spent.

Voice 3:

> The myriad Santas
> Are getting a bit tarnished.
> The big plastic one,
> In the center of town,
> Has been up since before Thanksgiv-
>   ing,

And his red coat
Is covered with the soot and grime
Of our ever-increasing production.

Voice 1:

The piped-in music
Is getting to be
Too familiar.

Voice 2:

The myriad lights
Are taken as
A matter of course.

Voice 3:

The busyness of the season
Almost makes us wish
That it were finished.

Narrator 1:

Such is the commonly thought
But unuttered cry in the streets.
The clerks in the store
Conceal beneath their smiling faces
Nerves that are almost
At the breaking point.

Narrator 2:

The shoppers
In the air of false Christmas spirit
Become impatient.
The advertised specials
And the unadvertised specials
Are not what they had expected.
The endless minutes of waiting

For purchases
And the free gift-wrapping
Cause them to become
Impatient and critical
In this time of supposed
Good will toward men.

Narrator 3:

Put away the gaudiness;
The chartreuse and shocking pink
Of the contemporary Santas.
Put away the brightness
Of a thousand shining candles.
Put away the rasping music
Of the organ with the ubiquitous trem-
    olo.
Put all of the Madison Avenue Christ-
    mas
Away.

Speaking Choir:

Why put this away?
Why bring us to this darkened church,
Where all is shadow?
We live in light!

Narrator 1:

We live in incandescent
Neon light.
But is this light the answer?
Perhaps those thousands
Before this modern age
Knew more of light
Than we poor ones today.

Perhaps the lantern's glimmer
Gave presagement
Of what was to come.
The darkened world
Was waiting for the light
Of God to burst upon
The darkness of the mind.

Narrator 2:

There was deep darkness
Of the world.
But deeper still was darkness
Of despair,
Bitter hatred,
Unfulfilled hope.

Speaking Choir:

But do not these exist today?
Despair,
Hatred,
Unfulfilled hope?
What can the past
Bring to us?

Narrator 3:

Such answers
Cannot always
Be formed in words.
They must be experienced,
Lived,
Shared.
We are but travelers
In an eternity of times.
We move too fast.

> The endless cartoons
> Of awkward and foolish men
> That we draw in our every action
> Need perspective.

Narrator 1:

> Perhaps if our world were darkened;
> Perhaps if we could stop our frenzied
>   pace
> Long enough to watch and wait,
> We could see ourselves as we really are:
> Men longing and seeking
> For a different light.
> Watch, then,
> And wait.
> Perceive thyself in meditation
> In the darkness of this night.

(All is silence. A low bell is heard in the distance. The watchman takes his place at stage left. He lights his lantern and begins to walk across the stage, as a watchman making his rounds. From the balcony, as if at a great distance, comes singing.)

Singing Choir:

> Watchman, tell us of the night,
> What its signs of promise are:

Watchman:

> Traveler, o'er yon mountain's height,
> See that glory-beaming star!

Singing Choir:

> Watchman, doth its beauteous ray
> Aught of joy or hope foretell?

Watchman:

> Traveler, yes; it brings the day,
> Promised day of Israel.

Singing Choir:

> Watchman, tell us of the night;
> Higher yet that star ascends:

Watchman:

> Traveler, blessedness and light,
> Peace and truth, its course portends.

Singing Choir:

> Watchman, will its beams alone
> Gild the spot that gave them birth?

Watchman:

> Traveler, ages are its own,
> And it bursts o'er all the earth!

Singing Choir:

> Watchman, tell us of the night,
> For the morning seems to dawn:

Watchman:

> Traveler, darkness takes its flight;
> Doubt and terror are withdrawn.

Singing Choir:

> Watchman, let thy wanderings cease;
> Hie thee to thy quiet home.

Watchman:

> Traveler, lo, the Prince of Peace,
> Lo, the Son of God, is come! [2]

(During the musical dialogue, the watchman completes his circuit. The lights are gradually focused on him. At the

completion of the dialogue he puts down his lantern and
rests on his staff. The lights go down until all again is in
darkness. The watchman is seated when the lights are out.)

Speaking Choir:

    Watchman, tell us of the night,

    Tell us of the Promised Day,

    The Prince of Peace,

    The Son of God.

    Tell us, what do these mean?

Narrator 1:

    The people that walked in darkness

    Have seen a great light:

    They that dwell in a land of the
        shadow of death,

    Upon them hath the light shined. . . .

    For unto us a child is born,

    Unto us a son is given:

    And the government shall be upon his
        shoulder:

    And his name shall be called

    Wonderful, Counselor, The mighty
        God,

    The everlasting Father, The Prince of
        Peace.[3]

Narrator 3:

    Long centuries ago people

    Walked in darkness.

    Knew not the way to go —

Speaking Choir:

    Long centuries ago:

    What of today?

Do *we* know the way to go?
Do *we* know where we are? —
Who we are?

Narrator 1: Son of man, I have made thee a watchman. . . .
Therefore hear the word at my mouth, And give them
warning from me.[4]

Speaking Choir:

We should listen? We should be watch-
men?
Are we worthy?

Narrator 1:

When I consider thy heavens, the work
of thy fingers,
The moon and the stars, which thou
hast ordained;
What is man, that thou art mindful of
him? . . .
For thou hast made him a little lower
than the angels,
And hast crowned him with glory and
honor.[5]

Speaking Choir:

We are a little lower than the angels?
We are crowned with glory and honor?

Narrator 2:

Arise, shine; for thy light is come,
And the glory of the Lord is risen upon
thee.
For, behold, the darkness shall cover
the earth,

And gross darkness the people:
But the Lord shall arise upon thee,
And his glory shall be seen upon thee.[6]

Narrator 1:

Prepare ye the way of the Lord,
Make his paths straight,[7]
For this child shall be called the
    prophet of the Highest:
To give light to them that sit in dark-
    ness, . . .
To guide our feet into the way of
    peace.[8]

Speaking Choir:

To guide our feet into the way of peace.
Could we have heard correctly?
To guide our feet into the way of
    peace?

Narrator 2:

Yes. . . . Since the beginning of time
God has sought to reconcile men;
Has sought understanding and love;
Has sought to guide men's feet in the
    paths of peace.

Narrator 1:

At the beginning God expressed Him-
    self.
That Personal Expression was with
    God and was God,
And He existed with God from the
    beginning.
All creation took place through Him,

And none took place without Him.
In Him appeared Life and this Life was
    the Light of mankind.
The Light still shines in the darkness,
    and
The Darkness has never put it out.[9]

Speaking Choir:

The darkness has never put it out?
And what of the light, watchman?
Is this the same light of which you
    speak?

Narrator 3:

The same light
From the very beginning of time!
The darkness has never put it out —
Even though from the beginning of
    time man rebelled
Against God's command.
Adam and Eve ate of the fruit of the
Tree of the knowledge of good and
    evil.
They alienated themselves from God!
God's fellowship with man was incom-
    plete
From that time forward.

Narrator 2:

Down through the ages there have been
    those who have
Rebelled against God.
Only a few remained faithful;
Only a few understood the glory of
    God;

      Only a few saw that light shining in
        the darkness.

Speaking Choir:

      But the few who saw the light –
      What did God do?

Narrator 3:

      God staged a miracle:
      The Miracle of the Manger.

Speaking Choir:

      What can this mean?
      The Miracle of the Manger?

Narrator 1:

      There was a virgin in the land of Israel
      Whose name was Mary.
      She was espoused to Joseph,
      Who was of the house of David.
      The angel, sent from God,
      Came to her and said:

(The lights come up on Mary, seated at stage right. Behind her stands an angel dressed in white. The angel seems to enfold Mary as they both look upward. The light intensifies during the following narration.)

Narrator 2: Hail, thou that art highly favored, the Lord is with thee: blessed art thou among women.[10] Fear not, Mary: for thou hast found favor with God. And, behold, thou shalt . . . bring forth a son, and shalt call his name Jesus. He shall be great, and shall be called the Son of the Highest; and the Lord God shall give unto him the throne of his father David: And he shall reign over the house of Jacob for ever; and of his kingdom there shall be no end.[11]

Soprano Solo: " The Magnificat "[12]

> (*The lights fade on the angel and Mary. The watchman stirs, picks up his lantern, and resumes his circuit. He goes first to stage left, stops, and appears to be looking for something. He then retraces his steps to stage right.*)

Narrator 3:
>   But the days continued
>   As days of darkness.
>   The iron hand of Rome
>   Ruled the world.
>   The mighty exalted themselves
>   At the expense of the humble and
>   meek.

Speaking Choir:
>   But what of God's miracle?
>   The miracle of the manger?
>   And what of the Light?

> (*The watchman's lantern illumines a large parchment decree which is written in Latin. The watchman puzzles over the wording of the decree as the narrator continues.*)

Narrator 1: And it came to pass in those days, that there went out a decree from Caesar Augustus, that all the world should be taxed. . . . And all went to be taxed, every one into his own city. And Joseph also went up from Galilee, out of the city of Nazareth, into Judea, unto the city of David, which is called Bethlehem, . . . to be taxed with Mary his espoused wife.[13]

Narrator 2: The Lord himself shall give you a sign; Behold, a virgin shall conceive, And bear a son, and shall call his name Immanuel, God with us.[14]

Narrator 3:

> And thou Bethlehem, in the land of Juda,
> Art not the least among the princes of Juda:
> For out of thee shall come a Governor,
> that shall rule my people Israel.[15]

Organ (*pp.*): " O Little Town of Bethlehem " " St. Louis "

Narrator 1:

> It was evening.
> Joseph was weary after the long, dusty,
> journey,
> Pulling the donkey after him.
> Mary, heavy with child,
> Had ridden the tiresome journey.
> They came to Bethlehem and stopped
> outside an inn.

(Joseph and Mary enter. Joseph knocks once on the door. He knocks again; the door opens, showing a lighted interior. A young man takes the message to the innkeeper, who talks to Joseph. He shrugs, and finally leads him out to the stable. The stable is not lighted or visible. One may see in the dusk a little of Mary's blue robe as she moves upstage.)

Narrator 2:

> An inn is a welcome place on a cold
> night.
> The brightness of the light is inviting,
> And there is warmth and jollity inside.
> There are voices and laughter,
> There is comradeship around the table.
> An inn is a welcome place on a cold
> night.
> If there is room.

Speaking Choir:

> If there is room!
> Was there no room in this inn?

Narrator 3:

> There was no room in this inn.
> There was only a stable,
> Dark and damp.
> The only warmth comes from the bod-
>   ies of cattle and sheep,
> And there is no one to give a word of
>   welcome.

Singing Choir: " O Little Town of Bethlehem " (Stanza 1)
                                                    " St. Louis "

(Choir continues humming as the narrator begins.)

Narrator 3: And so it was, that, while they were there, . . .
she brought forth her firstborn son, and wrapped him in
swaddling clothes, and laid him in a manger; because
there was no room for them in the inn.[16]

Singing Choir: " O Little Town of Bethlehem " (Stanza 2)
                                                    " St. Louis "

Narrator 1:

> In that city of David
> A miracle happened.
> If it had not been a miracle,
> It would have faded and been forgotten
>   by now.
> That night, so long ago,
> Transformed the world.
> For it brought together all men;
> Men of every degree,

> Every walk of life.
> God exalted the poor, the laborers, the
>   ignorant men,
> And kings left their palaces to come
>   and bow before
> A babe in a manger.
> The scholars and wise men left their
>   studies
> To travel to a stable
> And kneel on the stone floor.

Narrator 2:

> Thus, the light came back into the world.
> The Miracle of the Manger,
> God's hope — for God himself became
> Man; to live among us,
> To reconcile God with man
> And man with man.

Speaking Choir:

> Did man know about this miracle?
> Did it change man?

Narrator 2:

> The radiance of the light was faint at
>   first;
> Only a few knew what had come to
>   pass,
> Only a few cared.
> But we are told:

Narrator 1: There were . . . shepherds abiding in the field,
keeping watch over their flocks by night. And, lo, the
angel of the Lord came upon them, and the glory of the
Lord shone round about them; and they were sore afraid.[17]

(*A dim light appears upon the shepherds at stage right. It gradually intensifies.*)

Speaking Choir:
> Shepherds, humble shepherds.
> They saw the light?

Narrator 2:
> To the lowly, humble shepherds,
> Who spent their lives upon the hillside
> Watching over their flocks,
> Tired, with bruised feet and sore hands,
> Often cold and hungry —
> To these men of lowly station
> God sent a choir of angels
> Resplendent in robes of heavenly hue,
> Shining with a brilliant brightness,
> Brighter than anything they had ever
>   seen.
> To them the story of the miracle was
>   revealed.

Narrator 3: Fear not: for, behold, I bring you good tidings of great joy, which shall be to all people. For unto you is born this day in the city of David a Saviour, which is Christ the Lord. And this shall be a sign unto you; Ye shall find the babe wrapped in swaddling clothes, lying in a manger.[18]

(*Several angels appear to the shepherds. The brightness intensifies. The shepherds, awe-struck, kneel before the heavenly host.*)

Narrator 3: And suddenly there was with the angel a multitude of the heavenly host praising God, and saying,

> Glory to God in the highest,
> And on earth peace,
> Good will toward men.[19]

Speaking Choir:

> Glory to God in the highest,
> And on earth peace,
> Good will toward men.

Singing Choir: "While Shepherds Watched Their Flocks by Night" (Stanzas 1, 3, 4, and 6)   "Christmas"
(Shepherds cross stage slowly in the direction of the stable, which is still in darkness. The light fades as they move up, and we glimpse them starting to kneel.)

Narrator 1:

> The shepherds came —
> These men whose feet were bruised by
>   the sharp stones
> And whose hands were torn by the
>   brambles;
> Men who had spent all their lives out of
>   doors,
> Who walked alone in the darkness to
>   find a lost sheep.
> The shepherds had not read the
>   prophets.
> They were ignorant men;
> Yet they knew the Messiah was to
>   come.

Speaking Choir:

> The Messiah,
> The Light — in the darkness of the
>   world.
> Who else saw the Light?

Narrator 2:

> Tradition tells us there were
> Three wise men from the east —
> Members of the privileged class.
> Men who lived in luxury,
> Slept on couches of silk,
> Walked on rugs of deepest pile,
> Never hungered,
> Never suffered from the warmth of
>   summer or cold of winter;
> Scholarly men, who had read of the
>   prophets'
> Foretelling of the King to be born
> Who would save all mankind.

Narrator 3:

> For these three men
> God chose a star —
> One of the hundreds of the stars of the
>   heavens —
> And used that star to guide these men
> To Bethlehem
> To see the Light,
> To bring gifts to the Prince of Peace.

Narrator 1: Behold, there came wise men from the east to Jerusalem, saying, Where is he that is born King of the Jews? for we have seen his star in the east, and are come to worship him.[20]

Narrator 2: When Herod the king had heard these things, he was troubled, and all Jerusalem with him. . . . Then Herod, when he had privily called the wise men, inquired of them diligently what time the star appeared. And he sent them to Bethlehem, and said,[21]

Narrator 1: Go and search diligently for the young child; and when ye have found him, bring me word again, that I may come and worship him also.[22]

Narrator 2: When they had heard the king, they departed; and, lo, the star, which they had seen in the east, went before them, till it came and stood over where the young child was. When they saw the star, they rejoiced with exceeding great joy. And when they were come into the house, they saw the young child with Mary his mother, and fell down, and worshipped him.[23]

(Three kings begin to walk down the side aisle, cross the chancel, and move in the direction of the stable.)

Singing Choir: " We Three Kings of Orient Are "
                                                            " Kings of Orient "

(As the Wise Men begin to open their gifts, the light fades.)

Narrator 1: And when they had opened their treasures, they presented unto him gifts; gold, and frankincense, and myrrh,[24]

Narrator 2:
> It was at the manger
> That those of high degree were brought
>   down
> As the Wise Men bowed before the
>   young child,
> Offering their gifts.

Narrator 3:
> It was at the manger
> That those of low degree were exalted
> As the shepherds worshiped their King.

Narrator 1:

> Again, today,
> This miracle goes on,
> As rich men, ignorant men,
> Wise men, simple men,
> Those from the East,
> And those from the West,
> All races, all colors, and kinds
> Come together to worship their Lord,
> The Son of God,
> Born to a woman in a lowly stable,
> Born to mankind on this mother earth.

(*The members of the rhythmic choir, representing the races of mankind, enter from various places in the sanctuary and come together at stage center. During the singing of the hymn, they move with the music, ending in a tableau group around the manger.*)

Singing Choir: " In Christ There Is No East or West "
                                              " St. Peter "

(*As the choir finishes the hymn, the lights begin to come up on the stable. At first they are dim and show the Nativity only in shadowy outline.*)

Narrator 1: Thou shalt not harden thine heart, nor shut thine hand from thy poor brother: But thou shalt open thine hand wide unto him, and shalt surely lend him sufficient for his need.[25]

Speaking Choir:

> To give us enough for our need —
> Is this why the Light came?

Narrator 2:

> The coming of the Light
> Was to give renewed life to the world;
> That we might have life,
> And have it more abundantly.

Singing Choir: " What Child Is This? "   " Greensleeves "

(Lights on the stable brighten and come to full brilliance at the end of the music.)

Narrator 3:

> The Miracle of the Manger —
> The child, the mother, Joseph,
> The shepherds, the Wise Men,
> All men of good will.

Narrator 1:

> Will the Miracle happen anew
> To you, in your hearts?
> Will you prepare him room?

Singing Choir:

> " Silent Night! Holy Night! " (Stanzas 1, 2, 3, and 4)
> " Stille Nacht "

(For the final tableau, the shepherds are joined hand in hand to the Wise Men, and they to the people of the world. The last person in the series extends an outstretched arm to the worshipers, symbolizing that they are part of the worshiping host.)

Narrator 1:

> It is the miracle of the ages,
> This manger miracle.
> As time runs out each year
> We celebrate

The Advent of our Christ.
God hopes this year,
As he has in all the many years gone by,
To have Christ born in you.
Take away all semblance of pride,
Idle gossip,
Materialistic conformity,
Covetousness,
Cruel hatred,
The exaltation of self,
The alienation from God.

Speaking Choir:

Take away
Pride,
Gossip,
Conformity,
Covetousness,
Hatred,
Exaltation of self,
Alienation from God.

Narrator 1 (*organ plays pp.*):

Let kindness,
Tenderheartedness,
Forgiveness,
Take their place.
Let God's miracle
Happen to *you*.
On this winter night,
When our hearts have been warmed
By this re-enactment of the past,
Let us not depart
With only a visual memory.

(Organ plays mf. for the following)

Let us take Christ anew into our hearts,
Into our minds,
Into our lives.
Kindle in every home
The Spirit of his presence
Both now and forevermore.

Organ and Choir *(organ plays ff.)*: Amen.

Congregational Hymn: " Joy to the World "   " Antioch "

SOURCES

1. It is suggested that the organist improvise on or play the following numbers: "O Come, O Come, Emmanuel " ("Veni Emmanuel "); "Come, Thou Long-expected Jesus " ("Hyfry-dol "); "Lo, How a Rose E'er Blooming " ("Es Ist Ein Ros'"); "O Morning Star, How Fair and Bright " ("Frankfurt ").

2. *The Hymnbook,* Hymn 149, sung to the tune " St. George's, Windsor."

3. Isa. 9:2, 6.

4. Ezek. 3:17.

5. Ps. 8:3-5 (adapted).

6. Isa. 60:1-2.

7. Luke 3:4.

8. Luke 1:76-79.

9. John 1:1-5 (Phillips Translation).

10. Luke 1:28.

11. Luke 1:30-33.

12. *The Hymnbook,* Hymn 596.

13. Luke 2:1-5.

14. Isa. 7:14; Matt. 1:23.

15. Matt. 2:6.

16. Luke 2:6, 7.

17. Luke 2:8, 9.

18. Luke 2:10-12.
19. Luke 2:13-14.
20. Matt. 2:1-2.
21. Matt. 2:3, 7-8a.
22. Matt. 2:8b.
23. Matt. 2:9-11a.
24. Matt. 2:11b.
25. Deut. 15:7b-8a.

"ANGELS O'ER THE FIELDS"

The following may be used by boys and girls from primary age through senior high school as a service of worship prior to a lesson period. It may be augmented by the use of pictures or slides. The service includes an Advent hymn, an old French carol, and a simple Polish carol in anthem form. The entire group of boys and girls can be used as a speaking choir. The music selections should be changed as necessary so they are suitable to the age group that is using the service.

If it is desired, this service of worship may be used at the beginning of a longer service. To lengthen this service, the following plays are suggested:

Herod and the Magi, adapted by Anne Malcolmson from the miracle play *The Magi, Herod, and the Slaughter of the Innocents,* in *Seven Medieval Plays for Modern Players.* Houghton Mifflin Company.

The Flight into Egypt, by Thornton Wilder, from *One-Act Plays of Spiritual Power,* selected and edited by Fred Eastman. Walter H. Baker Co.

Call to Worship (*by the speaking choir*):
> Everywhere, everywhere, Christmas to-
> night. . . .
> The angels who welcome him sing
> from the height,
> "In the City of David, a King in his
> might."
> Everywhere, everywhere, Christmas to-
> night.[1]

93

Hymn: "Come, Thou Long-expected Jesus" "Hyfrydol"

Scripture (*by the speaking choir*): Luke 2:8-16 (RSV)

POEM

Shepherd 1:
> The night lies still upon the hill, broth-
> ers, brothers —

Speaking Choir:
> Aye, still — the night lies still.

Shepherd 2:
> Yon star hangs high in the blue-black
> sky, brothers, brothers —

Speaking Choir:
> Aye, high in the blue-black sky.

Shepherd 3:
> The flocks we fold from fright and
> cold, brothers, brothers —

Speaking Choir:
> Aye, safe — from fright and cold.

Shepherd 1:
> And like the sheep I'm down to sleep,
> brothers, brothers —

Speaking Choir:
> Aye, like the sheep — to sleep — to
> sleep.

Shepherd 2:
> Oh, wake! Oh, rise! In yonder skies
> There flames the gold of dawn, broth-
> ers —

Shepherd 3:

> Peace! Peace! Shall we be duped by
>   thee?
> The night is not half gone, brothers!

Speaking Choir:

> The night lies still,
> The stars hang high,
> The flocks are safe in the fold, brothers.
> Shall men like sheep
> Lie fast asleep
> When heaven's gates unfold, brothers?

Solo Voice:

> Wake, shepherds! Rise!
> Across the skies
> Glad hallelujahs ring, brothers!
> Those angels bright —
> They blind the sight —
> What mean the words they sing, broth-
>   ers? [2]

Anthems: "Angels We Have Heard on High"   "Gloria"
    "Infant Holy" [3]   Arr. by Reed-Carlton Young

LULLABY

Solo Voice:

> Jesus, baby, rest thee
> Soft on Mary's breast —

Speaking Choir:

> Holy, holy, holy —
> Babe on Mary's breast,

Solo Voice:

> Jesus, tender lambkin,
> Dear to shepherd heart —

Speaking Choir:

> Holy, holy, holy —
> Shepherd too thou art.

Solo Voice:

> Jesus, priceless treasure
> Of the sages' quest —

Speaking Choir:

> Holy, holy, holy —
> Kneel we to be blest.[2]

Anthem: " The Angels Sang a Gloria "[4]   Curry

Hymn: " Angels, from the Realms of Glory "
                                        " Regent Square "

Benediction

SOURCES

1. Phillips Brooks.
2. *Good Will Toward Men: A Musical Christmas Pageant,* by S. Franklin Mack and Alice Hudson Lewis. The Westminster Press, 1942.
3. *Anthems for the Junior Choir,* Book 4.
4. Church Music Review, No. 1602. The H. W. Gray Company, Inc.

III

"SHALL WE NOT
THY SORROWS SHARE?"

THE LENTEN SEASON IS A TIME WHEN PRAYER AND MEDITATION
are foremost in the mind of the Christian. It is the time
when the individual reflects on the work of Christ in the
world and the salvation that he brought to all men. While
the tenor of this season of the church year is for the most
part solemn, this does not mean that it is unimaginative.
Spiritual meaning can be effectively conveyed by the use of
various art forms, and the use of the arts at this time may
heighten the significance of the season.

During the Lenten season, in many churches the choir
presents a cantata or an oratorio. To interpret the meaning
of the choral service, slides of reproductions of great art have
been used, or prints of pictures have been displayed in an
adjacent room. We must always keep in mind that each person is an individual, and that what will be meaningful to
one may need further interpretation for another; hence it is
well to provide several ways to express the meaning of a
particular incident in the life of Christ and his church.

While the services in this section are tied to certain days
because of their context, they may be presented at any time
during Lent. It would be possible to create other services and
to present a series of dramatic episodes during the Lenten
period. The important thing is to add deeper meaning for
the persons who participate and for those who worship.

" A KING BEYOND ALL DOUBTING "

The service of worship that follows is designed for Palm Sunday, when it could be presented as a vesper service by the young people of the church, assisted by choirs of children and youth. The dramatic episode, which forms the main part of the service, may be presented by a speaking choir or by several narrators. Pantomime is effective in the three sequences of the shepherds, the disciples, and the villagers and merchants. If the scenes are posed, the shepherds should be costumed in rough garments and should indicate their understanding of the narrative by means of searching looks and gestures. The disciples should wear tunics, rough-textured robes, and sandals. The movements of the disciples should be uncertain, except for the movements of the two who go to carry out the Master's command. The villagers wear simple robes and headdresses. Some should carry water jars. The merchants are richly dressed, and at the beginning of their narration, can be examining their wares.

In this dramatic episode, as has been true of others in this collection, we have given brief suggestions that are intended only to indicate possibilities for staging. As far as possible, every effort should be made to fit the dramatization into the situation of the local church. If the church is fortunate enough to have rheostats, they could be used to suggest the intensity of the action as it develops. If they are not available, spotlights may be used.

The arrangement in this collection is for speaking choir, but other arrangements may be used depending upon the creativity of the director.

Call to Worship: " Blessed Is He Who Cometh " [1] Gounod

Hymn: " All Glory, Laud, and Honor " " St. Theodulph "

SCRIPTURE READING [2]

Speaking Choir: And when they drew near to Jerusalem, to Bethphage and Bethany, at the Mount of Olives, he sent two of his disciples, and said to them,

Solo 1: " Go into the village opposite you, and immediately as you enter it you will find a colt tied, on which no one has ever sat; untie it and bring it. If any one says to you, ' Why are you doing this? ' say, ' The Lord has need of it and will send it back here immediately.' "

Speaking Choir: And they went away, and found a colt tied at the door out in the open street; and they untied it. And those who stood there said to them,

Semi-Chorus 1: (*The speaking choir should be divided into two parts, thus making equally balanced choirs, Semi-Chorus 1 and Semi-Chorus 2.*)

" What are you doing, untying the colt? "

Speaking Choir: And they told them what Jesus had said; and they let them go. And they brought the colt to Jesus, and threw their garments on it; and he sat upon it.

Semi-Chorus 1: And many spread their garments on the road,
Semi-Chorus 2: And others spread leafy branches which they had cut from the fields.

Semi-Chorus 1: And those who went before

Semi-Chorus 2: And those who followed cried out,

Speaking Choir: " Hosanna! Blessed be he who comes in the name of the Lord! . . . Hosanna in the highest! "

Anthems: " Lift Up Your Heads " [3]   Wennerberg-Curry
          " From Bethany " [4]   Curry

DRAMATIC EPISODE: A King Beyond
All Doubting

(*Following the last anthem, the organist will improvise on its theme while the four groups in the dramatic episode enter the sanctuary in rhythmic procession and take their places in the chancel area. The shepherds pose on a slightly elevated platform at stage right. The villagers are at stage left and can be grouped around an improvised well. The merchants with their wares are seated upstage center. The disciples pose in front at stage right, some standing in small groups and others kneeling. As the speaking choir reads each sequence, an amber spotlight illuminates the group about which the narration is speaking. Each group exits down the center aisle at the end of the episode, during the singing of the hymn " Hosanna, Lord Hosanna."*)

Shepherd Sequence (*Three or four shepherds move from repose to animation during the reading of the stanzas*):

Light Voices:

> As we watched on the hillside green,
> Poor shepherds with our younglings,
> From far away we saw him come
> And move within our viewing.

Dark Voices:

> No sound he made as he walked by;
> We questioned at his going.

> But nought we found from anyone —
> It were as he were dying.

Disciple Sequence (*The group of twelve are clustered together at the beginning and move outward to allow the two who will bring the colt to go into the village*):

Speaking Choir:

> As we stood hushed outside the town
> Our Master we were heeding.

Dark Voices:

> Our nets we'd left beside the sea
> So we could do his bidding.

Speaking Choir:

> A strange request he made to us,
> Beyond our comprehension,
> That we should ride with him this day
> Into the blest Jerus'lem.

Duet (Dark Voices):

> We two were charged to loose the colt
> That yet no man had sat on.
> Though   questioned,   our   reply   was
>   given,
> " The colt for Christ to ride on."

Speaking Choir:

> In silence then the ride began,
> Soon silence was behind us.
> From out the village gate they ran
> To hail the King most glorious.

Village Sequence: (*While intent upon themselves at the beginning of the sequence, the villagers soon move to see the*

pageantry, which is coming into the city of Jerusalem.
They pass the merchants, who watch them with interest.)

Light Voices:

As we were at the village well,
Our daily work completing,
We heard a shout from out the wall
And rushed to see its causing.
A crowd, a song, a shout prolonged,
All raised their vibrant voices,
And gave to us the echoing words,
" Jerusalem rejoices! "

(Merchants join the villagers and pantomime the
following lines.)

Dark Voices:

As villagers rushed quickly past,
We listened to their shouting;
" Such clamor must announce," said
          we,
" A King beyond all doubting."
And so we came to see this King,
And left our wares untended,
For we must greet this King who comes
With such great pomp attended.
And at the gate we saw him come;
The King appeared dejected,
Though he was now the central one,
By followers protected.
And as they passed we sensed that he
Spoke with a voice that sighest,
But this was masked with tumult
          strong,

Speaking Choir:
>   Hosanna in the highest!

(The children's choirs enter the sanctuary waving palm branches and singing.)

Anthem: " Hosanna to the Son of David " [5]   Curry

Speaking Choir:
>   They hailed him King as he passed by,
>   They strewed their garments in the
>   road,
>   But they were set on earthly things,
>   And he on God.
>   They sang his praise for that he did,
>   But gave his message little thought;
>   They could not see that their souls'
>   good
>   Was all he sought.
>   They could not understand why he,
>   With powers so vast at his command,
>   Should hesitate to claim their rights
>   And free the land.
>   Their own concerns and this world's
>   hopes
>   Shut out the wonder of his news;
>   And we, with larger knowledge, still
>   His Way refuse.
>   He walks among us still, unseen,
>   And still points out the only way,
>   But we still follow other gods
>   And him betray. [6]

Hymn: " Hosanna, Loud Hosanna "   " Ellacombe "

Benediction

Choral Response: " We Would See Jesus; Lo! His Star Is Shining " (Stanza 5)   " Cushman "

SOURCES

1. *Anthems for the Junior Choir,* Book 1.
2. Mark 11:1-10.
3. Harold Flammer, Inc., No. 84, 113, SATB.
4. Harold Flammer, Inc., No. 84, 605, SATB with Junior Choir.
5. *Anthems for the Junior Choir,* Book 2.
6. " He — They — We," in " *Gentlemen — The King!* " by John Oxenham. Used by permission.

COME, BE A GUEST

The sacrament of the Lord's Supper has an inherent beauty and dignity and can speak to many without embellishment. There is, however, the danger that this service will be taken only as a re-enactment of a historical event, and will not be infused with meaning and power for our everyday living. The following service has been designed to point out the historical setting of the Sacrament and to carry it into contemporary life, so that each breaking of our bread may serve to remind us of the gift of Christ. As the presence of Christ was recalled to the disciples at Emmaus by the breaking of bread, so may every common meal which we eat become reminiscent of the divine Sacrament.

The narration and tableaux that are suggested here are to precede the service of Holy Communion. Such a service in this dramatic form would be appropriate for Maundy Thursday, or for the final evening of a conference or summer leadership training school. The Communion table, covered with a white cloth, is in the center of the chancel and is used for the first episode in the enactment of the Last Supper. The same table will later be used for the serving of the congregation. At one side of the chancel, on a raised platform, is a round table with three chairs for the Emmaus sequence. This setting could be copied from Rembrandt's *Supper at Emmaus,* which is noted in the service. For the last episode, a dining table set with goblets and place settings occupies the other side of the chancel on the nave level. If the posing of the episodes is not possible, slides may be used.

Prelude: " Lencten-Orison " [1]   Edmundson

Minister:

> What shall I render to the Lord
> for all his bounty to me?
> I will lift up the cup of salvation
> and call on the name of the Lord,
> I will pay my vows to the Lord
> in the presence of all his people.[2]

Anthem: " What Shall I Render to My God? " [3]   Lovelace

Minister: " Christ, our paschal lamb, has been sacrificed. Let us, therefore, celebrate the festival." [4]

Hymn: " O Son of Man, Our Hero Strong and Tender "
                                     " Charterhouse "

THE PROLOGUE

Narrator 1: Throughout the ages, man has spoken to man, and his words have become empty because they have been only of himself. Though man has been given the ability to think and to express his thoughts, too often these thoughts are only of himself. Words have been spoken by man that have become almost immortal, but these which have been so dignified have been submerged in a confusion of tongues and incoherent babblings. Ofttimes the trees of the wood have spoken with more enduring words than has man, and somehow, through creation, through the prophets of God, and even through some modern men, God has spoken. But his perfect speech has been communicated by his Son, our Lord and Savior Jesus Christ.

Narrator 2: Hebrews 1:1-4; 2:1-4, 9-11

EPISODE I

Hymn: " Bread of the World in Mercy Broken "
" Eucharistic Hymn "

(During the singing of this hymn, the twelve disciples take their places around the center table. Jesus is in the middle. On the table are a silver or pewter chalice and a loaf of bread. Grecian oil lamps may be at either end of the table. Suggestions for posing the picture may be derived from viewing Leonardo da Vinci's The Last Supper.[5]*)*

Narrator 1: Matthew 26:26-29

(During the reading of the Scripture, the bread is broken and the cup is lifted and passed.)

Anthem: " Wondrous Love "[6]   Paul Christiansen

Narrator 2: Hebrews 2:10-13

EPISODE II

Hymn: " Here, O My Lord, I See Thee Face to Face "
" Morecambe "

(During the singing of this hymn, the center tableau breaks, and the three persons to be used in the Emmaus sequence take their places at the round table on the platform.)

Narrator 1: Luke 24:13-15, 28-31

(The sanctuary is in darkness during the first part of the reading. At the beginning of verse 28, the candle on the table is lighted so that the faces of the three men can be seen. A dim light can be used for further illumination. During the remainder of the reading, the bread is broken

and given. For arrangement and costuming, see the Rembrandt painting.[7])

Anthem: " Come, O Thou Traveler Unknown " [8]   Noble

Narrator 2: Hebrews 2:14-18

EPISODE III

Hymn: " Be Known to Us in Breaking Bread "

" St. Flavian "

(During the singing of this hymn, the second tableau dissolves. A family take their positions at the third table, the father standing at the head. He lights candles on the table and breaks and passes the bread during the singing of the anthem.)

Narrator 1: Luke 14:15-24

Anthem: " Draw Us in the Spirit's Tether " [9]   Friedell

Narrator 2: Hebrews 3:1-6

THE SACRAMENT OF HOLY COMMUNION

Hymn: " Ah, Dearest Jesus, How Hast Thou Offended "

" Herzliebster Jesu "

(During the hymn, the family exit. The elements are brought in to the center table for serving to the people.)

Minister: The Invitation to Holy Communion

Anthem: " The Sacrament Divine " [10]   Curry

Minister: The Words of Institution
The Giving of the Bread and the Cup

Hymn: " A Parting Hymn We Sing "   " Schumann "

Benediction

SOURCES

1. St. Cecilia Series, No. 699. The H. W. Gray Company, Inc.
2. Ps. 116:12-14.
3. Canyon Press, Inc., 1955, SATB.
4. I Cor. 5:7-8a.
5. American Library Color Slide Company, Inc., No. 3818.
6. Augsburg Publishing House, No. 1140, SATB.
7. American Library Color Slide Company, Inc., No. 770.
8. Church Music Review, No. 205. The H. W. Gray Company, Inc.
9. *Ibid.,* No. 2472.
10. *Ibid.,* No. 2530.

THE CRUCIFIXION

The moving poem by James Weldon Johnson is the basis for this Good Friday service. The impact of the service is dependent upon the feeling that is put into the reading by the speaking choir and the soloists. Much of the meaning of the service will depend upon the timing, the precision, and the colors that are applied to the written words.

It is suggested that this dramatic reading be presented in the chancel. At the center of the chancel is a mound of grass behind which is a receptacle for the cross, which is placed by Simon. At one side of the chancel, behind the mound, is the singing choir. Opposite the singing choir are the speaking choir and the soloists. The chancel steps or a ramp could be used for an approach to the green mound. At the beginning of the folk sermon, during the singing of "All in the April Evening," the lights are dimmed. A blue gelatine is inserted in the frame of the spotlight to suggest darkness. During the reading of the words on page 112, "And they take my blameless Jesus," the lights brighten until the reading "And Jesus, my lonesome Jesus," page 115, at which time the lights are dimmed. There should be complete darkness when the choir finishes humming "Were You There When They Crucified My Lord?"

Interpretative music could be played on the organ throughout the entire folk sermon. The use of sound effects, particularly for the thunder, would heighten the meaning of the entire service.

Prelude: " Meditation on ' Ah, Dearest Jesus ' " [1]

Crüger-Dickinson

" Six Chorale Preludes on ' When Jesus on the
Cross Was Bound ' " [2]   Scheidt

Prologue (*by the Narrator*): Isaiah 52:13 to 53:12

Anthems: " Jesu, Lord Jesu " [3]   Stainer

" All in the April Evening " [4]   Robertson

THE FOLK SERMON: The Crucifixion [5]

Speaking Choir:

> Jesus, my gentle Jesus,
> Walking in the dark of the garden —
> The Garden of Gethsemane,
> Saying to the three disciples:

Solo 1:

> Sorrow is in my soul even unto death;
> Tarry ye here a while and watch with
> me.

Speaking Choir:

> Jesus, my burdened Jesus,
> Praying in the dark of the Garden —
> The Garden of Gethsemane. Saying:

Solo 1:

> Father, Oh Father, this bitter cup,
> This bitter cup, let it pass from me.

Speaking Choir:

> Jesus, my sorrowing Jesus,
> The sweat like drops of blood upon his
> brow,

Talking with his Father while the three
disciples slept,
Saying:

Solo 1:

Father, Oh Father, not as I will,
Not as I will, but let thy will be done.

Light Voices:

Oh, look at black-hearted Judas —
Sneaking through the dark of the Gar-
den —
Leading his crucifying mob.

Dark Voices:

Oh, God! Strike him down!

Light Voices:

Why don't you strike him down,
Before he plants his traitor's kiss
Upon my Jesus' cheek?

Speaking Choir:

And they take my blameless Jesus
And they drag him to the Governor,
To the mighty Roman Governor,
Great Pilate seated in his hall —
Great Pilate on his judgment seat, said:

Solo 2:

In this man I find no fault.
I find no fault in him.
And Pilate washed his hands.

Speaking Choir:

But they cried out, saying:

Light Voices:
> Crucify him!

Light and Medium Voices:
> Crucify him!

Speaking Choir:
> Crucify him!
> His blood be on our heads.

Light Voices:
> And they beat my loving Jesus,

Dark Voices:
> They spit on my precious Jesus;

Light Voices:
> They dressed him up in a purple robe,

Dark Voices:
> They put a crown of thorns upon his
>   head,
> And they pressed it down —

Speaking Choir:
> Oh, they pressed it down —
> And they mocked my sweet King Jesus.

(*Choir hums " All in the April Evening " as the crowd,
with Simon carrying the cross, comes down the center aisle.
The humming continues through the line, " Oh, look how
they done my Jesus."*)

Solo 3:
> Up Golgotha's rugged road I see my
>   Jesus go.
> I see him sink — beneath the load,
> I see my drooping Jesus sink.

Light Voices:

>   And they laid hold on Simon, Black
>   Simon,

Dark Voices:

>   Yes, Black Simon;
>   They put the cross on Simon, and
>   Simon bore the cross.

(Simon places cross behind a mound in the center of the chancel.)

Speaking Choir:

>   On Calvary, on Calvary, they crucified
>   my Jesus.
>   They nailed him to the cruel tree,

Solo 4:

>   And the hammer!

Trio (Light Voices):

>   The hammer!

Light Voices:

>   The hammer! Rang through Jerusa-
>   lem's streets.

Light and Medium Voices:

>   The hammer!

Dark Voices:

>   The hammer!

Speaking Choir:

>   The hammer! Rang through Jerusa-
>   lem's streets.

Solo 5:

> Jesus, my lamb-like Jesus,
> Shivering as the nails go through his
> hands;

Solo 6:

> Jesus, my lamb-like Jesus,
> Shivering as the nails go through his
> feet.

Solo 5:

> Jesus, my darling Jesus,
> Groaning as the Roman spear plunged
> in his side;

Solo 6:

> Jesus, my darling Jesus,
> Groaning as the blood came spurting
> from his wound.

Solo 7:

> Oh, look how they done my Jesus.

Light Voices:

> Mary, weeping Mary,
> Sees her poor little Jesus on the cross.
> Mary, weeping Mary,
> Sees her sweet baby Jesus on the cross,
> Hanging between two thieves.

Solo 8:

> And Jesus, my lonesome Jesus,
> Called out once more to his Father, say-
> ing:

Solo 1:

> My God, My God, Why hast thou for-
> saken me?

Solo 8:

> And he dropped his head and died.

Speaking Choir:

> And the veil of the temple was split in
> two,
> The midday sun refused to shine,

Dark Voices:

> The thunder rumbled and the light-
> ning wrote
> An unknown language in the sky.
> What a day! Lord, what a day!
> When my blessed Jesus died.

(Choir hums "Were You There When They Crucified My Lord?" and continues until all lights are off.)

Solo 8:

> Oh, I tremble, yes, I tremble,
> It causes me to tremble, tremble,
> When I think how Jesus died;
> Died on the steeps of Calvary,
> How Jesus died for sinners,
> Sinners like you and me.

(All lights are off. From the balcony comes a voice.)

Voice: Revelation 21:1-7; 22:20-21

Choral Response: "Christ, We Do All Adore Thee" [6]

Dubois

(The choir exits as rapidly as possible, preferably through side exits. The lights go slowly on, and the congregation leaves silently.)

SOURCES

1. St. Cecilia Series, No. 625. The H. W. Gray Company, Inc.
2. Edited by Walter Buszin. Concordia Publishing House, OC339.
3. Sir John Stainer, from *The Crucifixion*.
4. G. Schirmer, Inc., Curwen Edition, 60976.
5. From *God's Trombones,* by James Weldon Johnson. Copyright, 1927, by The Viking Press, Inc.; 1955, by Grace Nail Johnson. It must not be used for public readings, dramatic recitals, etc., when any fee is paid to the reader or readers or used on the radio or on television, or reprinted or reproduced in any way, without obtaining formal permission in advance from The Viking Press, Inc.
6. From *The Seven Last Words of Christ,* by Theodore Dubois.

" THE TERRIBLE MEEK "

The production of this drama written for the furtherance
of world peace can well be presented in the chancel of the
church. Although the action is almost entirely in darkness,
the set design is important and should be worked out with
great care and detail and with the architectural arrangement
of the sanctuary in mind. The play has been produced effectively without a set and in modern costume.

For those who desire a set, suggestions can be found in the
published version.[1] There should be a backdrop of gray sky,
with three crosses and a rocky hillock as set pieces. At the
end of the dramatization the crosses may be silhouetted by
backlighting. The hillock should occupy the center of the
chancel and should be connected to one side of the chancel
by an ascending platform. Papier-mâché rocks, clumps of
grass, and a few branches will help create the setting, but it
is essential that a feeling of barrenness be achieved. Lighting
plays an important part in the unfolding of the drama, and
well-timed and authentic sound effects are extremely important. It is imperative that the congregation be prepared for
a different approach to the crucifixion and that the characters be portrayed by sensitive actors. This is not a drama to
be produced as a first attempt by an amateur group, but
should be a result of continued growth in Christian drama.

We have suggested that the drama be preceded by a brief
service of worship, with the choir carrying the Biblical narrative up to the crucifixion. As the organ plays an interlude,
the lights in the sanctuary are slowly dimmed until all is
darkness. From the balcony or rear of the church, a narrator

reads the Scripture lesson. When the narrator has finished,
nine brazen notes, far off and dissonant are heard, and the
drama begins.

After the presentation of the drama, the lights remain up
for the silent recessional by the choir. The lights then are
gradually dimmed and the choir sings the response from the
narthex.

Prelude: " In Manus Tuas, Domine " [2]   Peeters

Silent Processional

Introit: " None Other Lamb, None Other Name "

" All Hallows "

RESPONSIVE SENTENCES

Minister:

Fear not, for I have redeemed you;
I have called you by name, you are
mine.

People:

When you pass through the waters I
will be with you;
and through the rivers, they shall not
overwhelm you.

Minister:

Thus says the Lord, the King of Israel
and his Redeemer, the Lord of hosts:
" I am the first and I am the last;
besides me there is no god." . . .

People:

> I have swept away your transgressions
> > like a cloud,
> > and your sins like mist;
> > return to me, for I have redeemed you.

Unison:

> > Sing, O heavens, for the Lord has done
> > > it;
> > > shout, O depths of the earth;
> > break forth into singing, O mountains,
> > > O forest, and every tree in it!
> > For the Lord has redeemed Jacob,
> > > and will be glorified in Israel.[3]

Prayer: O God, from whom all holy desires, all good counsels, and all just works do proceed: Give unto thy servants that peace which the world cannot give; that our hearts may be set to obey thy commandments, and also that by thee, we, being defended from the fear of our enemies, may pass our time in rest and quietness; through the merits of Jesus Christ our Savior. Amen.[4]

Hymn: " God of Compassion, in Mercy Befriend Us "
                                          " O Quanta Qualia "

Lenten Prayers

Anthems: " Sing Alleluia Forth "[5]   Thiman
        " A Carol for Palm Sunday "[6]   Curry
        " Go, Congregation, Go! "[7]   Antes-Dickinson

Scripture: John 19:17-30

Drama: " The Terrible Meek "[1]   Charles Rann Kennedy

Benediction

Choral Response: "None Other Lamb, None Other Name"
"All Hallows"

SOURCES

1. *The Terrible Meek,* by Charles Rann Kennedy. Walter H. Baker Co.

2. *Ten Chorale Preludes on Gregorian Hymns,* Peters Edition, No. 6090. C. F. Peters Corporation.

3. Isa. 43:1b-2a; 44:6, 22, 23.

4. *The Book of Common Worship* (1946) (The Board of Christian Education of the Presbyterian Church in the United States of America), pp. 372–373.

5. Novello & Co., Ltd. (The H. W. Gray Company, Inc.), No. 989.

6. *Anthems for the Junior Choir,* Book 4.

7. Early American Moravian Church Music, No. 6. The H. W. Gray Company, Inc.

IV

"LOVE IS COME AGAIN"

EASTER, THE MOST IMPORTANT DAY IN THE MEANING OF THE Christian church, is prepared for intensively by the observance of Lent but is only briefly celebrated as a particular day. In part, this may be due to the fact that people have become so involved with " churchgoing " during Lent that Easter is a release for them. While we grant that Easter can well speak for itself, at least in theological and doctrinal terms, there are some who need a re-enactment of this important day in dramatic fashion. Accordingly, the services of worship in this section have been developed to state unequivocally the meaning of Easter.

In the Christian church it has become traditional to welcome this glad day with an early-morning service of worship reminiscent of the historical day when the good news of the resurrection was proclaimed to the followers of Jesus. In some communities this early-morning service has been presented by the young people of the congregation. The first service in this chapter, " An Easter Dawn Service," has been created with them in mind. The pageant of " The Resurrection," by Rosamond Kimball, and the service entitled " The Continuing Christ " in this book could also be used for an early-morning service. " An Easter Round of Carols " could

well be presented on Easter afternoon for the entire congregation, thus carrying forward the importance of this day
in the life of the church. It is imperative in all these services
that the triumphant note be asserted, for this is the true
meaning of the day.

AN EASTER DAWN SERVICE

The service that follows is designed for an outdoor setting, although it may be presented effectively in the church sanctuary. There is silence as the worshipers gather before the service. At the hour appointed for worship, the two narrators take their places at opposite sides of an improvised chancel.

The service as outlined is dependent upon the rhythmic choir, which interprets the meaning of Easter through symbolic movements. The choir is composed of twelve girls divided into four groups. At the beginning of the service they enter, carrying two long strips of purple cloth, which they extend to make a cross. As the events progress, the cloth, which has been used to represent the actual form of a cross, is intertwined among the members of the choir, symbolizing the victory of Christ over the cross and the unity in Christ that binds all mankind together.

Narrator 1: And God said, " Let there be light "; and there was light. And God saw that the light was good; and God separated the light from the darkness. God called the light Day, and the darkness he called Night. And there was evening and there was morning, one day.[1]

Narrator 2: And when the sabbath was past, Mary Magdalene, and Mary the mother of James, and Salome, bought spices, so that they might go and anoint him. And very early on the first day of the week they went to the tomb when the sun had risen. . . . And entering the tomb, they saw a young man sitting on the right side, dressed in a white robe; and they were amazed. And he said to them, " Do not be amazed; you seek Jesus of Nazareth, who was crucified. He has risen, he is not here; see the place where they laid him." [2]

Introit (*singing choir*): " This Is the Day of Light " (Stanza 1)   " Swabia "

    This is the day of light:
    Let there be light today;
    O Dayspring, rise upon our night,
    And chase its gloom away.

Brass Quartet: " Jesus Christ Is Risen Today "
                     " Easter Hymn "

(*During the music the members of the rhythmic choir assume kneeling positions in groups of three at the outward extensions of the cross that is formed from two long strips of purple cloth. The center person in each group of three holds an end of the cross-cloth. As each group of three rises, the center person releases the cloth.*)

Trumpet Fanfare [3]

Narrator 1:

    Souls in the east, awake.
    Make ready to meet the dawn.
    The sun of God is rising,
    The bridegroom from his chamber,
    Rejoicing as a strong man
    To run his race.
    He is risen.

(*The three in the east arise and move arms slowly upward. They are dressed in flowing robes of gold.*)

Eastern Voices: Alleluia! He is risen!

Trumpet Fanfare

Narrator 2:

Souls in the north, awake.
Souls of the dead, remember,
He goeth before you into Galilee.
Is he here? Is he there?
He is everywhere;
He is risen.

(*The three in the north arise and move arms slowly upward. They are dressed in flowing robes of silver.*)

Northern Voices: Alleluia! He is risen!

Trumpet Fanfare

Narrator 1:

Souls in the south, awake.
Winter is dead, Spring lives.
Purple and gold the crocus comes.
The beauty of the world returns;
He is risen.

(*The three in the south arise and move arms slowly upward. They are dressed in green.*)

Southern Voices: Alleluia! He is risen!

Trumpet Fanfare

Narrator 2:

Souls in the west, awake.
Souls of the years to come,
Christ guide you on your way
Into this world, and out again.
He knows the way to come and go —
Comes with a star, goes with a cross,
And comes again with a triumph;
He is risen.

(*The three in the west arise and move arms slowly upward. They are dressed in blue.*)

Western Voices: Alleluia! He is risen!

All Voices:

> Awake, all souls that sleep.
> Across the year but once or twice
> Can men hear angels calling.
> Heed that *first* trumpet, nor await the
>   last.
> The resurrection moment soon is past.
> Life calls again, to all that would be
>   living,
> He is risen.
> Alleluia! He is risen! [4]

Interlude (*singing choir*): " This Is the Day of Light "
  (Stanza 2)   " Swabia "

> This is the day of rest:
> Our failing strength renew;
> On weary brain and troubled breast
> Shed Thou Thy freshening dew.

(*During the singing of this stanza, the four groups move into one circle around the cross so that the four colors alternate: gold, blue, silver, green, etc. It will be necessary for some members of the group to step over the cloth in order to take their proper places in the circle. The group face outward and indicate with the movement of their arms the strength that comes from God to his people. The cross remains on the chancel floor, symbolizing the victory of Christ over the cross.*)

Narrator 1: Ephesians 2:4-7 (RSV)

Interlude: "This Is the Day of Light" (Stanza 3)

"Swabia"

> This is the day of peace:
> Thy peace our spirits fill;
> Bid thou the blasts of discord cease,
> The waves of strife be still.

(During the singing of this stanza, four choir members lift the strips of cloth from the floor. The choir then proceed to intertwine the two strips about their waists. One person becomes the connecting link between the two pieces, so that a continuous strip is formed. Snaps for attaching the cloth to the gowns of the choir members may be used to keep the cloth in place.)

Narrator 2: Ephesians 2:13-18 (RSV)

Interlude: "This Is the Day of Light" (Stanza 4)

"Swabia"

> This is the day of prayer:
> Let earth to heaven draw near:
> Lift up our hearts to seek thee there;
> Come down to meet us here.

(During the singing of this stanza, the group move to a kneeling position and lift hands in prayer. If snaps are not used to hold the cloth in place, each member may lift one hand in prayer, using the other hand to hold the cloth around the waist in an unobtrusive manner.)

Narrator 1: Ephesians 2:19-22 (RSV)

Interlude: "This Is the Day of Light" (Stanza 5)

"Swabia"

> This is the first of days:
> Send forth Thy quickening breath,

And wake dead souls to love and praise,
O Vanquisher of death!

(During the singing of this stanza, the group move in single file down the center aisle, with the intertwined purple cloth joining them together.)

Brass Quartet: " Thine Is the Glory " [5]   " Judas Maccabeus "

Anthem: " Thine Is the Glory " [6]   Handel-Curry

Benediction

Sources

1. Gen. 1:3-5.
2. Mark 16:1-6.
3. Fanfares may be adapted from anthems such as " Hosanna to the Son of David," *Anthems for the Junior Choir,* Book 2, or " A Carol for Palm Sunday," *Anthems for the Junior Choir,* Book 4.
4. The selections by Narrator 1, Narrator 2, and All Voices are from " An Easter Reveille," by John R. Slater. Used by permission of the author.
5. *The Hymnbook,* Hymn 209.
6. *Anthems for the Junior Choir,* Book 3.

"THOU RISEN LORD"

This service of worship could well be used as an Easter dawn service or as a vesper service on Easter afternoon. It is based on a pageant of the resurrection arranged by Rosamond Kimball.[1] While there are a number of suggestions made in the printed dramatization, the following suggestions are added as alternatives.

On page 5 of the printed copy, where Selection II of the Passion music is cued, an alternative is the substitution of dramatic tension music, building it up carefully in order to increase the volume gradually without drowning out the reader's voice. As the reader finishes saying, "And the sun was darkened and the veil of the temple was rent in the midst," quickly develop into full organ and for about thirty seconds create cacophony suggestive of turmoil. One method of doing this is to place the left foot at right angles to the lower pedal notes, playing as many notes as possible simultaneously to create the sound of thunder. While this is being done, a wind effect is created by rapidly progressing thirds, fourths, or fifths in the treble register, ascending and descending while swell shades operated with the right foot contribute to the varying intensity of sound. The ability to create a good wind effect with the right hand alone would enable the organist to weave a harmonic effect with the left hand. Usually a flute or diapason combination adapts itself to wind imitation more readily than do strings or reeds; however, the organist may wish to do a bit of experimenting beforehand. As this effect nears its close, begin to reduce the volume, and return to a soft organ to accompany the reader again, taking up Selection II of the Passion music as the reader says, "And when Jesus had cried out with a loud voice. . ."

The tomb may be constructed by making a frame box large enough to accommodate two adults. Chicken wire should be affixed over the box, and branches and greenery should be interwoven into the wire. If these materials are not available, use rock paper procured from a wallpaper store, or crepe paper. The top of the tomb may be covered with artificial grass, and flowers and greenery may be inserted into the roof.

Inside the tomb, a board covered with a sheet may be used for the bench on which the angels sit. A blue light should be wired inside the tomb and used when the angels appear. The back of the tomb should be open so the angels can enter it.

The front of the tomb should be on an angle. A frame of wood covered with cardboard should be painted to represent the stone or covered with rock paper. This should be placed downstage so that the priests may roll it to seal the tomb. It must be light enough in weight so that the angels can move it from the inside when the lines give the cue.

Prelude: " The Strife Is O'er " [2]   H. Alexander Matthews

Hymn: " Jesus Christ Is Risen Today "   " Easter Hymn "

Scripture (*by the speaking choir*):
(*Dark voices read Mark 15:43-47 and light voices Mark 16:1-8.*)

Anthem: " ' Christ the Lord Is Risen Today ' " [3]   Young

Prayer

Hymn: " O Sons and Daughters, Let Us Sing! "
                                " O filii et filiae "

Offertory: " O What the Joy and the Glory Must Be " [2]
H. Alexander Matthews

DRAMA: " THE RESURRECTION: AN EASTER SERVICE " [1]

Prelude (*narrator and organ*): The Crucifixion

Episode I: The Audience Chamber of Pontius Pilate

Episode II: The Guard at the Sepulcher

Episode III: The Women at the Sepulcher

Episode IV: The Disciples at the Sepulcher

Hymn: " The Day of Resurrection! "   " Lancashire "

Benediction

Postlude: " In Thee Is Gladness " [4]   Bach

SOURCES

1. *The Resurrection: An Easter Service,* by Rosamond Kimball. Walter H. Baker Co.

2. *Twelve Choral Preludes on Familiar Hymn Tunes.* Oliver Ditson Co., Inc. (Theodore Presser Co.).

3. *Anthems for the Youth Choir,* Book 1.

4. *Historical Organ Recitals,* Vol. II. G. Schirmer, Inc.

THE CONTINUING CHRIST

We must be careful in the Christian church to make contemporary the story of Jesus and to translate his presence into our daily lives. The short dramatization that follows is an attempt to move a little beyond the historical Easter and to create an imaginary conversation among some of the young people who lived in Jesus' day. It is also hoped that young people will see the risen Christ as our constant companion today and understand the meaning of his Kingdom on earth.

This dramatization was presented as a service of worship for a junior high department on Easter. It can be presented in the chancel or in an assembly room and does not require the use of curtains or an elaborate stage setting. One or two wooden benches, some pottery water jars, a few palm trees, and some flowers will suggest the setting of a courtyard. Costumes should be simple but in good taste. Darker fabrics could be used for the men, and the women could be clothed in lighter colors. Properties should be carefully chosen. Some research should be done by the producing group to ascertain the type of properties that are needed. Suggestions for properties are included in the script. Characters are as follows:

PETER'S NIECE, *the hostess*
DAUGHTER OF THE WOMAN OF SAMARIA
SECOND MAID FROM SAMARIA
YOUNG SHEPHERD
MAID FROM THE HOME OF JOSEPH OF ARIMATHEA
NEPHEW OF JAMES AND JOHN

DAUGHTER OF CLEOPAS OF EMMAUS
DAUGHTER OF JAIRUS
BOY WHO SHARED HIS LOAVES AND FISHES
SON OF THE CENTURION
SINGING VOICE OFFSTAGE

Organ Prelude

Call to Worship: The angel of the Lord has declared to us,
" Do not be afraid; for I know that you seek Jesus who was
crucified. He is not here; for he has risen, as he said. Come,
see the place where he lay. Then go quickly and tell his
disciples that he has risen from the dead, and behold, he is
going before you to Galilee; there you will see him. Lo, I
have told you." [1]

Hymn: " Jesus Christ Is Risen Today "   " Easter Hymn "

Prayer of Dedication (*in unison*): O God, help us to walk
with Jesus and have his mind. May we follow him all the
way, even unto Calvary. Show us the meaning of the cross,
and cast its shadow over our lives. Help us to be coura-
geous enough to face the fate of the cross and to give our
lives for the cause he loved. We know that all those who
sincerely try to live as he lived and to teach his message
will also find a cross atop the hill. Strengthen us, O God,
to follow this way with confidence and faith. Grant that
through our suffering and sacrifice we may understand
the Easter message and claim true discipleship with him.
O may the Easter glory rest upon us today, and may new
life be born within us. In the victory of thy Son we go forward to victory in our own life, and he dwells with us
always. May he transform us as he transformed his first
disciples, and may we spread his truth abroad today, in
his Name. Amen. [2]

SCRIPTURE LESSON [3]

(*By the Speaking Choir*)

Girls: Now on the first day of the week Mary Magdalene came to the tomb early, while it was still dark, and saw that the stone had been taken away from the tomb. So she ran, and went to Simon Peter and the other disciple, the one whom Jesus loved, and said to them,

Solo: They have taken the Lord out of the tomb, and we do not know where they have laid him.

Boys: Peter then came out with the other disciple, and they went toward the tomb. They both ran, but the other disciple outran Peter and reached the tomb first; and stooping to look in, he saw the linen cloths lying there, but he did not go in. Then Simon Peter came, following him, and he went into the tomb; he saw the linen cloths lying, and the napkin, which had been on his head, not lying with the linen cloths but rolled up in a place by itself. Then the other disciple, who reached the tomb first, also went in, and he saw and believed; for as yet they did not know the scripture, that he must rise from the dead. Then the disciples went back to their homes.

Girls: But Mary stood weeping outside the tomb, and as she wept she stooped to look into the tomb; and she saw two angels in white, sitting where the body of Jesus had lain, one at the head and one at the feet. They said to her,

Two Boys: " Woman, why are you weeping? "

Solo Girl: She said to them, " Because they have taken away my Lord, and I do not know where they have laid him."

Boys: Saying this, she turned round and saw Jesus standing, but she did not know that it was Jesus. Jesus said to her, "Woman, why are you weeping? Whom do you seek?"

Girls: Supposing him to be the gardener, she said to him, "Sir, if you have carried him away, tell me where you have laid him, and I will take him away."

Boys: Jesus said to her, "Mary."

Girls: She turned and said to him in Hebrew, "Rabboni!" (which means Teacher).

Boys: Jesus said to her, "Do not hold me, for I have not yet ascended to the Father; but go to my brethren and say to them, I am ascending to my Father and your Father, to my God and your God."

Girls: Mary Magdalene went and said to the disciples, "I have seen the Lord"; and she told them that he had said these things to her.

Hymn (or Anthem): "Thine Is the Glory"⁴

"Judas Maccabeus"

Offering

DRAMATIC EPISODE

Narrator: Today our class wants to share with you some of the thoughts and feelings of a few young people who lived in the days when Jesus was on earth. Some of these individuals are described in the Bible; others are imaginary persons whom we think could have been in the group, meeting in the courtyard of Peter's house near Jerusalem and discussing the events of the first Easter. After those taking part in this scene have quietly left the stage, we hope that you in the worshiping congregation will also leave quietly, thinking of the continuing Christ and his message for us today.

Peter's Niece (*seated on bench sewing*): These are strange times in which we live! Our elders apparently think we young people know very little about what goes on. They seem to forget that we hear many of their conversations. Besides, wherever you go in the city you hear people talking about it.

Daughter of the Woman of Samaria: I know. This is the first time I have been to Jerusalem, but my mother and others in our village of Samaria, who count themselves disciples of Jesus, thought that they had to find out what was really happening. There were so many different stories flying around. Why, some people even said that your Uncle Peter had deserted Jesus and denied knowing him when he most needed friends at his trial! None of us could believe that. We remembered when Jesus came to our village and sat on the side of the well as he talked to my mother. That conversation made a great difference in our home and village. Of course I always loved my mother, although it was hard to understand the things she did — and her quick temper. But after she met Jesus, she became beautiful in character as well as in behavior.

Second Maid from Samaria: Yes, and do you remember how your mother introduced so many people of our village to Jesus?

Daughter of the Woman of Samaria: That's right. And we all remember Peter and the disciples who were with Jesus. Peter later admitted he didn't like us Samaritans at that time, and he was disturbed to find Jesus so friendly to us.

But later Peter often visited our house. We just knew he couldn't deny Jesus; he loved him so deeply.

Peter's Niece: But now you know that Uncle Peter did deny Jesus and ran away from the trial! He will never cease to be ashamed of that.

Young Shepherd (*carrying a crook*): I couldn't help hearing what you said. My father came to Jerusalem for the same reason that the Samaritans did. He let me come with him because he had told me so much about the night when Jesus was born that I felt that I too had been with my father and the other shepherds who went to see the baby at Bethlehem. We were with the crowd, watching from afar, as the Romans crucified Jesus. It was awful!

Maid from the Home of Joseph of Arimathea: My master, Joseph of Arimathea, told his wife about it, and I listened too. Even to hear about it was dreadful, but to see it must have been so awful that I should think you would never forget it.

Young Shepherd: I never shall!

Maid from the Home of Joseph of Arimathea: I helped to prepare the spices my master put on the body of Jesus before he and the others laid the Christ in my master's new tomb. My master felt sorry that he had not been more open in his support of Jesus when Jesus was alive. All of us wondered what it meant when we heard that the great stone had been rolled away and the tomb was empty!

Nephew of James and John (*with a fishing net*): You should have heard my Uncle John when he came back from the empty tomb! He made me wish I had gone with him, because he told of the angels who said that Jesus is risen —

not dead! I remember when Jesus used to visit our house.
I liked to follow him around and listen to his stories. He
never seemed to feel that young people are unimportant.
Indeed, it seemed as though he depended on us to help
him do things. Whenever he visited our house, the whole
atmosphere seemed happier. I loved to hear Jesus laugh!

Peter's Niece: Yes, I loved to hear him laugh too, and to
watch his face glow when he smiled!

Daughter of Cleopas (*sifting grain*): I think that I am the
luckiest of all the group here, for I saw Jesus after he was
raised from the grave. My father, Cleopas, brought Jesus
to our house for supper, and at first we didn't recognize
him. You see, all of us, including my father, were so sad
over the death of the Master that we couldn't think of anything else. My father and his friend walked almost all the
way from Jerusalem to Emmaus with Jesus, talking to
him. Jesus explained how the prophets and he himself had
foretold his coming, his death, and his resurrection. The
way Jesus described it, my father said, filled him with new
hope; and there was something about the voice of the
speaker that made my father's heart thrill! I know what
my father meant, because when our guest said grace for
us at the table, I just had to open my eyes and look at him.
And then I found myself thinking, It is our Master, Jesus!
Now he is here with us, and all our sadness will go! But
before I could say anything, he had finished grace, and
like that, he was gone! But by that time all of us knew
that we had been with the Lord, and that even if we
couldn't see him, his spirit was right there with us. From
that day on, I have never felt alone, for I have felt that
Jesus walks with me.

Daughter of Jairus: I know what you mean, even if I haven't seen Jesus since he was raised from the grave. You remember that when I was a small girl I was very sick and everyone, including my parents, thought I was dead. Jesus came to our house at the request of my father, Jairus, and Jesus said: " She is not dead. She sleeps." He took me by the hand and called my name, and immediately I was very much alive! If you have ever heard Jesus call *you,* and if you have looked into his face as I did, you can never be alone again. You *know* he is your friend and that he can and will help you whenever you need him.

Boy Who Shared His Loaves and Fishes (*approaching with the centurion's son and carrying a fishing net*): You don't mind if we join you, do you? We were just passing the gate and couldn't help hearing the daughter of Jairus speak. I felt I just had to come and join the conversation because, you know, it was my lunch of loaves and fishes Jesus used to feed the five thousand people who listened to him talk about the Kingdom of God. Maybe I was too young to understand *all* he had to say, but the fact that he used my lunch to help all those people is something that I shall never forget. It has made me want to use whatever I have to help other people. After spending most of that day with him, I have felt that he is with me all the time, and it makes a difference in the way I try to do things. I can't wait until I go to live in his Father's Kingdom! It sounds so wonderful.

Son of the Centurion: Why do you say you can't *wait* to go to God's Kingdom? The way Jesus talked to my father, my father thinks we can be a part of God's Kingdom here and now. If we choose to follow the way of Jesus, the way you say you do day by day, we *are* part of God's Kingdom.

Of course, my father and I are Romans, and so perhaps we do not know as much about God's Kingdom as you Jews do. You know, my father went to Jesus once when a servant was very sick to ask if Jesus would come to our house to cure him. But Jesus didn't have to come to the house. He just told my father to go home, because the man had been made well. Some time later, my father took me to see Jesus. I am so glad he did, because Jesus has been my personal friend ever since. Even though I don't *see* him every day, I know *he* lives.

Peter's Niece: Listen! Do you hear someone singing?

(*A voice offstage sings " I know That My Redeemer Liveth." *[5])

Nephew of John: I think that is my Uncle John singing! Perhaps he's seen the risen Jesus again. Let's go and ask him about it so that we can join him in saying: I *know* that my Redeemer lives, and because he lives, we too shall live eternally.

(*All go out in twos and threes, talking quietly, looking for the singer.*)

Sources

1. Matt. 28:5-7.
2. *The Hymnal for Youth,* p. 354. The Westminster Press, 1941.
3. John 20:1-18.
4. *Anthems for the Junior Choir,* Book 3, p. 48.
5. From *The Messiah,* by George Frederick Handel.

AN EASTER ROUND OF CAROLS

Easter is a joyous time, and its gladness is well-reflected in the carols that have been written about it. This service could be presented on Easter afternoon, or the various episodes could be used on consecutive Sundays in Lent for departmental services of worship. If the latter is done, the series should build to a climax on Easter. This same general plan may be followed for similar services built around another great theme of the church year. A number of art masterpieces are suggested for use in the service. Reproductions of them may be shown with an opaque projector, or slides may be secured or made, or the scenes may be posed. There are perhaps more reservations about posing scenes that represent the events of Easter than in posing those that tell of Christ's birth. The feeling of the local church must be taken into consideration in deciding how the pictures will be presented. Some churches may wish to use an intense light to signify the presence of Christ, while others may use a human figure with his face partially hidden. In making our decisions, perhaps it is well to remember that we do not hesitate to use an inanimate doll to represent the Christ-child, who came to give life to the world. Therefore we should not think it inappropriate to use a human representation of the man Christ, particularly if we take seriously the fact that each of us is spiritually created in the image of God.

Whatever decisions are made concerning the manner of presentation, it is our hope that the service will speak to man anew of the power of Christ, our risen Lord.

Prologue: " When It Was Yet Dark " [1]   Shaw

Carol: "Love Is Come Again " [2]   Old French melody

EPISODE I

Narration: " Easter: St. John 20:1–20 " [3]   de Banke

Call to Worship: " Christ Is Risen " [4]   Kettring

Picture: *Holy Women at the Tomb* [5]   Ender

Carol: " The World Itself Keeps Easter Day " [6]
Piae Cantiones

EPISODE II

Narration: " Tell the Disciples " [7]   Author unknown

Picture: *Peter and John, Running to the Tomb* [8]   Bernaud

Carol: " Christ the Lord Is Risen " [9]   Old German melody

EPISODE III

Narration: " An Easter Canticle " [10]   C. H. Towne
          " The Resurrection " [11]   Brunini

Picture: *The Resurrection* [12]   della Francesca

Carol: " We Will Be Merry " [13]   Praetorius-Curry

EPISODE IV

Narration: " The Walk to Emmaus " [14]   Cowper

Picture: *Supper at Emmaus* [15]   Rembrandt

Carol: " Easter Carol " [16]   French carol

EPISODE V

Narration: Matthew 28:16–20

Picture: *The Ascension* [17]   Coleman

Carol: "Wondrous Works " (Part II) [18]
                    Traditional English melody

SOURCES

1. *Moods in Poetry,* by Cécile de Banke, Pamphlet III. Walter H. Baker Co.
2. *The Oxford Book of Carols,* No. 149.
3. de Banke, *op. cit.,* p. 28.
4. *Anthems for the Mixed Choir.*
5. Cynthia Pearl Maus, *Christ and the Fine Arts,* p. 431.
6. *The Oxford Book of Carols,* No. 150.
7. Maus, *op. cit.,* p. 447.
8. *Ibid.,* p. 434.
9. *The Oxford Book of Carols,* No. 148.
10. de Banke, *op. cit.,* p. 37.
11. James Morrison, ed., *Masterpieces of Religious Verse,* No. 643.
12. The Frick Collection.
13. *Anthems for the Junior Choir,* Book 1.
14. *The Story of Jesus in the World's Literature,* by Edward Wagenknecht (Creative Age Press, Inc., 1946), p. 452. Farrar, Straus & Cudahy, Inc.
15. The New York Graphic Society.
16. *The Oxford Book of Carols,* No. 147.
17. Coleman Collection. Holt, Rinehart and Winston, Inc.
18. *The Oxford Book of Carols,* No. 72.

"O WORD OF GOD INCARNATE"

No one in the Christian church would dispute the fact that the Bible is central in all that we do or say, and, as a group of early divines said, it is " the only infallible rule of faith and practice." While all the services in this book are Biblically centered, there are often times when certain portions of Scripture can be emphasized and made more relevant by the use of the arts.

The Bible can be used as an organizing theme for a series of special services planned by the local church. In connection with this series, it might be well to plan an exhibit of Bibles, using particularly those Bibles which demonstrate the art of printing and illustration. An exhibit of paintings on Biblical subjects could also be included. It is important that we attempt to communicate the various meanings of the Biblical narrative in a number of ways.

Some of the services in this section are amplifications of the Biblical narrative as the stories are conceived in different settings. This has been done to show that the Bible speaks in an immediate context, and that it can be comprehended in different ways by different people. It is of the utmost importance that we continually seek ways in which the Bible may speak to us in our present situation, and it is hoped that these services will arouse new ideas for this kind of presentation. Basic to all of this is the conviction that the Holy Spirit may speak in various ways, so it is imperative that we provide channels through which this may be accomplished.

THE CREATION

This service of worship makes use of the intensely personal interpretation of the Biblical narrative of creation as it has been portrayed in a Negro folk sermon by James Weldon Johnson. The narrative is presented by soloists and a speaking choir as the elements of creation, enumerated below, rhythmically portray the story. Lighting and costuming are essential to the production, and while the suggestions included here for costuming have a tendency toward the actual outward appearance of the elements, in some situations it would be wise to attempt to convey the meaning in a more symbolic way.

For the production, the chancel or stage should include three platforms. Behind each of these platforms is a set piece painted to represent the nebulous background of creation. The choirs, both singing and speaking, are vested and occupy opposite sides of the chancel. The elements of creation are represented as follows:

Sun: a girl wearing a white drape; she holds a yellow circle.

Moon: a girl wearing a white drape and holding a white circle.

Stars (two or three): girls wearing blue drapes spangled with stars; stars made of cardboard covered with metallic foil hang from the participants' fingers.

Earth: a girl wearing an aqua drape; a large, papier-mâché globe is held low in front.

Grass: a small girl wearing a green drape, grass crown, and grass fingers.

Flowers: two or three small girls wearing green drapes with floral head pieces.

Pine Tree: a girl wearing a brown drape and holding pine branches.

Oak Tree: a girl wearing a brown drape and holding oak leaves.

Rivers and Lakes: four to six girls wearing blue and green drapes, hands joined as they move rhythmically in an intertwining sequence.

Rainbow: girls wearing drapes of rainbow colors.

Fish, Fowl, Beasts, and Birds: a group of nine small girls dressed in leotards and wearing yard-square scarves attached at the waist and wrist in the following colors: Fish, green and orchid scarves; Fowl, gray and blue scarves; Beasts, brown and black scarves; Birds, yellow, red, and blue scarves.

Man: a tall, slim young man of ruddy complexion clothed in beige shorts.

The standards behind the platforms are made of beaverboard or light plywood. The platforms are fourteen inches high so that the complete tableaux may be seen. Three spotlights are needed, each one controlled by a projectionist. At the appropriate place in the narration the elements of creation take their places as follows:

Platform One, stage right: Sun, Grass, and Flowers.

Platform Two, stage center: Man (behind him is placed a representation of a Bible open at Genesis).

Platform Three, stage left: Pine Tree, Oak Tree, Moon.

In front of Platform Two: Earth; and at either side of this platform, Stars.

In front of the three platforms: Rivers, Lakes, Fish, Fowl, Beasts, Birds, and the Rainbow, moving rhythmically.

PROLOGUE

Hymn: " For the Beauty of the Earth "   " Dix "

Poem: " God " [1]

THE FOLK SERMON [2]

(*Presented in six scenes using narrator, speaking choir, singing choir, and rhythmic choir. The music to be used may be live or taped, according to the equipment of the church or auditorium used for the service.*)

Hymn-Anthem: " The Spacious Firmament on High "
                                      " Creation "

Narrator:

And God stepped out on space,
And he looked around and said:
I'm lonely —
I'll make me a world.

(*Light on the center platform with open Bible during the reading of the above narration.*)

Speaking Choir:

And as far as the eye of God could see
Darkness covered everything,

Blacker than a hundred midnights
Down in the cypress swamp.

(Complete darkness during the above lines.)

Narrator:

Then God smiled,
And the light broke,
And the darkness rolled up on one side,
And the light stood shining on the
    other,
And God said: That's good!

*(There is an alternation of darkness and light according to
the lines of the above section.)*

Speaking Choir:

Then God reached out and took the
    light in his hands,
And God rolled the light around in his
    hands
Until he made the sun;

*(The Sun moves rhythmically from a kneeling position
and takes her place on Platform One.)*

Narrator:

And he set the sun a-blazing in the
    heavens.
And the light that was left from mak-
    ing the sun
God gathered it up in a shining ball
And flung it against the darkness,
Spangling the night with the moon and
    stars.

(The Moon moves quickly to Platform Three, and the Stars, with graceful rising and falling motions, take their places between the platforms.)

> Then down between
> The darkness and the light
> He hurled the world;
> And God said: That's good!

(The Earth moves with thrusting motions and takes her place, kneeling in front of Platform Two. During the next sequence, the various elements move rhythmically as the soloists speak words about them. The Earth raises the globe upward during the last phrases. There is a yellow spotlight on Platform One and a blue spotlight on Platform Three.)

Speaking Choir:
> Then God himself stepped down —

Solo 1:
> And the sun was on his right hand,

Solo 2:
> And the moon was on his left;

Solo 3:
> The stars were clustered about his head,

Solo 4:
> And the earth was under his feet.

Speaking Choir:
> And God walked, and where he trod
> His footsteps hollowed the valleys out
> And bulged the mountains up.

Narrator:
> Then he stopped and looked and saw
> That the earth was hot and barren.

So God stepped over to the edge of the
     world
And he spat out the seven seas —

Speaking Choir:

He batted his eyes, and the lightnings
     flashed —
He clapped his hands, and the thunders
     rolled —
And the waters above the earth came
     down,
The cooling waters came down.

*(From behind the standards there is an alternation of light
and dark simulating lightning. This alternates with
thunder.)*

*(Grass and Flowers take their places on Platform One and
the Oak and Pine on Platform Three.)*

Narrator:

Then the green grass sprouted,
And the little red flowers blossomed,
The pine tree pointed his finger to the
     sky,
And the oak spread out his arms,
The lakes cuddled down in the hollows
     of the ground,
The rivers ran down to the sea;

*(The Lakes and Rivers take a circuitous path across the
chancel. There is a green light on the platforms, which
changes to white during the next three lines.)*

Speaking Choir:

And God smiled again,
And the rainbow appeared,
And curled itself around his shoulder.

(The Rainbow moves across the chancel in an undulating fashion.)

Narrator:

> Then God raised his arm and he
> > waved his hand
> Over the sea and over the land,
> And he said: Bring forth! Bring forth!

(Fish, Fowl, Beasts, and Birds come rapidly down the center aisle. The chancel is bathed in green and blue light.)

> And quicker than God could drop his
> > hand,
> Fishes and fowls
> And beasts and birds
> Swam the rivers and the seas,
> Roamed the forests and the woods,
> And split the air with their wings.

(Birds and other creatures move among the Rivers and the Lakes, the Flowers and the Trees. They then disperse to the extreme sides of the chancel, leaving only the Sun, the Moon, the Stars, and the Earth in a central position.)

> And God said: That's good!

Speaking Choir:

> Then God walked around,
> And God looked around
> On all that he had made.

Solo 1:

> He looked at his sun,

Solo 2:

> And looked at his moon,

Solo 3:

> And he looked at his little stars;

Solo 4:

> He looked on his world
> With all its living things,

Speaking Choir:

> And God said: I'm lonely still.

*(During the above, there is a yellow light on Platform One
and a white light on Platform Three. These gradually fade
until there is a dim light on the chancel during the next
lines.)*

Narrator:

> And God sat down —
> On the side of a hill where he could
>   think;
> By a deep, wide river he sat down;
> With his head in his hands,
> God thought and thought,
> Till he thought: I'll make me a man!

Speaking Choir:

> Up from the bed of the river
> God scooped the clay;
> And by the bank of the river
> He kneeled him down;

Narrator:

> And there the great God Almighty
> Who lit the sun and fixed it in the sky,
> Who flung the stars to the most far cor-
>   ner of the night,
> Who rounded the earth in the middle
>   of his hand;

Speaking Choir:
>This Great God,
>Like a mammy bending over her baby,
>Kneeled down in the dust
>Toiling over a lump of clay
>Till he shaped it in his own image;

>(*At this point, all lights are off. Man enters and the lights gradually come up.*)

Narrator:
>Then into it he blew the breath of life,
>And man became a living soul.

Speaking Choir: Amen, Amen.

>(*Lights begin to go down as Man stretches his arms upward and outward.*)

EPILOGUE

Prayer: " A Prayer for the Sacrament of Beauty " [3]

Hymn: " This Is My Father's World "   " Terra Patris "

SOURCES

1. Cynthia Pearl Maus, *Christ and the Fine Arts,* p. 557.

2. James Weldon Johnson, " The Creation," in *God's Trombones.* Copyright, 1927, by the Viking Press, Inc., 1955, by Grace Nail Johnson. The poem must not be used for public readings, dramatic recitals, etc. when any fee is paid to the reader or readers or used on the radio or on television, or reprinted or reproduced in any way, without obtaining formal permission in advance from The Viking Press, Inc.

3. Maus, *op. cit.,* p. 564.

THE WORD SINGS

The psalms have been used for centuries as the basis for much of the music of the church. The service of worship that follows relies heavily on the psalms and their paraphrases that have come down through the centuries. However, it also includes other hymns and anthems which allude to other portions of Scripture. The Bible is in many ways a singing word, and it is often through song that the individual's spirit is lifted up toward God.

This service, while general in character, could well be used for a community hymn festival. It is divided into the three elements of worship: adoration, confession, and thanksgiving, and as a whole is a sermon on hymnology. It may serve to point up some of the meaning behind the hymns that we sing and perhaps make us more conscious of the wealth of Biblical and theological concepts that are included in our church hymnals.

The service is arranged for a large chorus of adult choirs and youth or children's choirs. Congregational singing is also included. The arrangement of " The Old Hundredth Psalm Tune " is for congregation and choirs. The youth choir could sing alone one of the stanzas in this anthem. Youth or children's choirs could also sing the melody of the first theme in " Praise, Thanksgiving, Glory, Honor."

Prelude: " Beside Still Waters " [1]   Bingham
   (based on a figure from " Dominus regit me ")

Introit: " Now Let All the Heavens Adore Thee " [2]   Bach

Processional: " Processional for Organ " [3]   Martin Shaw
   (based on hymn tune " Lobe den Herren ")

ADORATION

Hymn: " Praise Ye the Lord "   " Lobe den Herren "

Minister: David also commanded the chiefs of the Levites to appoint their brethren as the singers who should play loudly on musical instruments, on harps and lyres and cymbals, to raise sounds of joy. . . . So all Israel brought up the ark of the covenant of the Lord with shouting, to the sound of the horn, trumpets, and cymbals, and made loud music on harps and lyres.[4]

Narrator 1: From almost its very beginning, the church has been one of the foremost patrons of the arts. The early Christian churches were decorated with mosaics that represented the characters and stories of the Bible by means of bits of glass. Setting these bits of glass into place was a tedious task, but the result was one of warmth and even mystery as the colors glowed in the dark interior of the church. The over-all design of the mosaic depended upon the ability of the eye to weld the various pieces together; yet each piece was necessary and contributed to the ulti- mate form of the mosaic. But let us consider another kind of mosaic — that which cannot be seen by the eye, but nonetheless is a gathering of bits from here and there, welded into one form. It is the mosaic of praise that has come down to us through the centuries, and that pictures, through words and music, the great song of the ages.

Narrator 2: It is spring. The Palestinian shepherd is alone on the hillside as the dulling pinks of the sunset become the haze of the evening. The darkness gathers in the budding trees, and the stars begin to push through the black loam of the sky. In his wonderment, it is conceivable that the shepherd might voice the words of the psalm:

Speaking Choir:

> Bless the Lord, O my soul!
> O Lord my God, thou art very great!
> Thou art clothed with honor and maj-
> esty,
> > who coverest thyself with light as
> > with a garment,
> who hast stretched out the heavens like
> a tent,
> who hast laid the beams of thy cham-
> bers on the waters,
> > who makest the clouds thy chariot,
> > who ridest on the wings of the wind,
> who makest the winds thy messengers,
> fire and flame thy ministers.
> Thou didst set the earth on its founda-
> tions,
> > so that it should never be shaken.[5]

Narrator 1: So the word of God sang through a shepherd; it was paraphrased over a hundred years ago, and continually sings today through the words of the following hymn.

Hymn: " O Worship the King All Glorious Above "

"Lyons "

Narrator 2: The music of the psalms was transferred by the early colonists of our country into *The Bay Psalm Book*, the first book to be published in English in the New World. It bears the place and date of Cambridge, Massachusetts, 1640. It may seem amusing to us to think of those early congregations singing eleven or twelve stanzas of a psalm in antiphonal form, with the leader, or precentor, intoning one phrase and the congregation answering with the same phrase. Listen as the choirs sing stanzas set to one of those early psalm tunes.

Anthem: " O God of Hosts " [6]   " York "-Barlow

Narrator 1: So the word of God sang through the pages of *The Bay Psalm Book,* and even today we sing almost each week the altered tune of " Old Hundredth," which has endured through the centuries. Its majesty and greatness reflect the being of God and offer to him the praise of men.

Anthem (*combined choirs and congregation*):
"The Old Hundredth Psalm Tune " [7]
                      Vaughan Williams

CONFESSION

Narrator 1: Albert Schweitzer has said, " Joy, sorrows, tears, lamentation, laughter — to all these, music gives voice, but in such a way that we are transported from the world of unrest to a world of peace, and see reality in a new way, as if we were sitting by a mountain lake and contemplating hills and woods and clouds in the tranquil and fathomless water." [8]

Narrator 2: And the bringing of our troubles and our cares to God has been voiced in the music of the ages as the confessions of a contrite heart are given to God.

Speaking Choir:
>Have mercy on me, O God, according
>   to thy steadfast love;
>According to thy abundant mercy blot
>   out my transgressions.
>Wash me thoroughly from my iniquity,
>   and cleanse me from my sin!

For I know my transgressions,
and my sin is ever before me.

Quartet 1:

Against thee, thee only, have I sinned,
and done that which is evil in thy
sight,
so that thou art justified in thy sentence
and blameless in thy judgment.

Quartet 2:

Behold, I was brought forth in iniquity,
and in sin did my mother conceive
me.
Behold, thou desirest truth in the in-
ward being;
therefore teach me wisdom in my se-
cret heart.

Quartets 1 and 2:

Purge me with hyssop, and I shall be
clean;
wash me, and I shall be whiter than
snow.
Fill me with joy and gladness;
let the bones which thou hast broken
rejoice.
Hide thy face from my sins,
and blot out all my iniquities.

Speaking Choir:

Create in me a clean heart, O God,
and put a new and right spirit within
me.

> Cast me not away from thy presence,
> and take not thy holy Spirit from me.
> Restore to me the joy of thy salvation,
> and uphold me with a willing spirit.[9]

Narrator 1: These words have been cast in a different way in the words of our next hymn. Let us sing with understanding and meaning as we make our confession to Almighty God.

Hymn: " God, Be Merciful to Me "   " Redhead, No. 76 "

Narrator 1: Our lives can be renewed by the power of God. As we have asked forgiveness for our sins, so we can be renewed by the Spirit of Christ. In a hymn of deep confession and yearning, we hear and relive the work of Christ in the lives of others and in our lives. Listen as these words recall to us the work of Christ.

Singing Choir:
" Dear Lord and Father of Mankind " (Stanza 1)

                         " Rest "

Narrator 2: Reclothe us in our rightful minds as Jesus did the demoniac.

Speaking Choir: And they came to Jesus, and saw the demoniac sitting there, clothed and in his right mind, the man who had had the legion; and they were afraid.[10]

Singing Choir:
" Dear Lord and Father of Mankind " (Stanza 2)

                         " Rest "

Narrator 2: Let us rise up and follow Christ as did those fishermen of Galilee.

Speaking Choir: And Jesus said to them, " Follow me and I will make you become fishers of men." And immediately they left their nets and followed him.[11]

Singing Choir:
" Dear Lord and Father of Mankind " (Stanza 3)

" Rest "

Narrator 1: Let us, in our lives, come apart to pray to God.

Speaking Choir: In these days he went out into the hills to pray; and all night he continued in prayer to God.[12]

Narrator 1: As we sing together the last two stanzas of this hymn, may the Spirit of Christ come upon us to aid us in our work in the world.

Hymn:
" Dear Lord and Father of Mankind " (Stanzas 4, 5)

" Rest "

THANKSGIVING

Narrator 1: The confessions of a contrite heart are a necessary part of the Christian life, but this life is also one of continual thanksgiving. St. Ambrose, centuries ago, reminded Christians that no duty is more urgent than that of returning thanks.

Narrator 2: True thanksgiving does not occupy a certain season, or a certain day, or a certain hour, but it is our constant appointment with God.

Narrator 1: " Stand still, think of the wonders of God." [13]

Narrator 2: Stand still and think. Think of the passing seasons and all the beauty they bring us. Think of all the blessings of God, and then give thanks.

Anthem: " A Thanksgiving Carol " [14]   Wolle-Curry

Narrator 1: Men in past generations have given thanks to God for his gifts of knowledge, courage, and strength; for his guidance and direction in their lives; for deliverance from trouble.

Narrator 2: The psalmist has expressed the thanksgiving of the people of God in this way:

Speaking Choir:
> O give thanks to the Lord, for he is
>   good;
>   for his steadfast love endures for ever!
> Let the redeemed of the Lord say so,
>   whom he has redeemed from trouble
> and gathered in from the lands,
>   from the east and from the west,
>   from the north and from the south. [15]

Narrator 1: Travelers have received guidance along the weary road and give their thanks unto the Lord.

Quartet 1:
> Some wandered in desert wastes,
>   finding no way to a city to dwell in;
> hungry and thirsty,
>   their soul fainted within them.
> Then they cried to the Lord in their
>   trouble,
>   and he delivered them from their dis-
>   tress;
> he led them by a straight way,
>   till they reached a city to dwell in.

Speaking Choir:

> Let them thank the Lord for his stead-
> fast love,
>> for his wonderful works to the sons
>> of men!
> For he satisfies him who is thirsty,
>> and the hungry he fills with good
>> things.[16]

Singing Choir:

"Almighty Father, Strong to Save" (Stanza 2)

"Melita"

Narrator 2: Prisoners have received light in their cells, and by the power of God, their guilt has been covered.

Quartet 2:

> Some sat in darkness and in gloom,
>> prisoners in affliction and in irons,
> for they had rebelled against the words
> of God,
>> and spurned the counsel of the Most
>> High.
> Their hearts were bowed down with
> hard labor;
>> they fell down, with none to help.
> Then they cried to the Lord in their
> trouble,
>> and he delivered them from their dis-
>> tress;
> he brought them out of darkness and
> gloom,
>> and broke their bonds asunder.

Speaking Choir:

Let them thank the Lord for his steadfast love,
for his wonderful works to the sons
of men!
For he shatters the doors of bronze,
and cuts in two the bars of iron.[17]

Singing Choir: "Melita"

O Christ, the friend of sinful men
Come visit us with love again,
And by the freedom of Thy Name
Restore men from a life of shame.
Be near them with Thy strength and
power,
And guard them in their life's dark
hour.

Narrator 1: Those who were without the light of reason
have received integration and a healthful personality by
the healing Spirit of God.

Quartet 3:

Some were sick through their sinful
ways,
and because of their iniquities suf-
fered affliction;
they loathed any kind of food,
and they drew near to the gates of
death.
Then they cried to the Lord in their
trouble,
and he delivered them from their dis-
tress;

he sent forth his word, and healed
    them,
  and delivered them from destruction.

Speaking Choir:

Let them thank the Lord for his stead-
    fast love,
  for his wonderful works to the sons
    of men!
And let them offer sacrifices of thanks-
    giving,
  and tell of his deeds in songs of joy! [18]

Singing Choir: " Melita "

O Spirit, who in troublous days,
Gives healing to our foolish ways;
Be near us now and give us power
To heal our minds in this dark hour.
Renew in us clear thoughts that we
Again may offer praise to Thee.

Narrator 2: Seafarers rejoice in wonders they have seen in
the deep, the calming of great storms, and the safe return
to port.

Quartet 4:

Some went down to the sea in ships,
  doing business on the great waters;
they saw the deeds of the Lord,
  his wondrous works in the deep.
For he commanded, and raised the
    stormy wind,
  which lifted up the waves of the sea.

They mounted up to heaven, they went
down to the depths;
their courage melted away in their
evil plight;
they reeled and staggered like drunken
men,
and were at their wits' end.
Then they cried to the Lord in their
trouble,
and he delivered them from their dis-
tress;
he made the storm be still,
and the waves of the sea were hushed.
Then they were glad because they had
quiet,
and he brought them to their desired
haven.

Speaking Choir:
Let them thank the Lord for his steadfast love,
for his wonderful works to the sons
of men!
Let them extol him in the congregation
of the people,
and praise him in the assembly of the
elders.[19]

Singing Choir:
"Almighty Father, Strong to Save" (Stanza 1)
"Melita"

Speaking Choir:
Whoever is wise, let him give heed to
these things;

let men consider the steadfast love of
the Lord.[20]

Singing Choir:
" Almighty Father, Strong to Save " (Stanza 4)

" Melita "

Minister: Prayer of Thanksgiving

Anthem: " Psalm 107 " [21]   Stanton

EPILOGUE

Narrator 1: Few of us will ever write hymns or anthems that
will become part of the tradition of the church, yet we
all can make our own mosaic of praise. Just as the artist
combined the small bits of glass to form his mosaic, so we
can combine our hearts and voices in the praise of God.
May our mosaic combine the brilliance and the glowing
tones that our hearts and minds give us as we sing praise
to the Lord.

Anthem: " Praise, Thanksgiving, Glory, Honor " [22]

Bechler-Dickinson

Narrator 2: Then I looked, and I heard around the throne
and the living creatures and the elders the voice of many
angels, numbering myriads of myriads and thousands of
thousands, saying with a loud voice, " Worthy is the Lamb
who was slain, to receive power and wealth and wisdom
and might and honor and glory and blessing! " And I
heard every creature in heaven and on earth and under
the earth and in the sea, and all therein, saying, " To him
who sits upon the throne and to the Lamb be blessing and
honor and glory and might for ever and ever! " [23]

Hymn: " Blessing and Honor and Glory and Power "

" O Quanta Qualia "

SOURCES

1. Carl Fischer, Inc., P1247.
2. Oliver Ditson Co., Inc. (Theodore Presser Co.), No. 332–14563.
3. J. B. Cramer and Company, Ltd., London, Set 7, No. 1.
4. I Chron. 15:16, 28.
5. Ps. 104:1-5.
6. *Anthems for the Adult Choir.* The Westminster Press, 1960.
7. Oxford University Press, New York, 1953.
8. Albert Schweitzer, *J. S. Bach,* Vol. I, pp. 338–339. The Macmillan Company, 1950.
9. Ps. 51:1-12.
10. Mark 5:15.
11. Mark 1:17-18.
12. Luke 6:12.
13. Job 37:14 (Moffatt).
14. *Anthems for the Junior Choir,* Book 3, p. 20.
15. Ps. 107:1-3.
16. Ps. 107:4-9.
17. Ps. 107:10-16.
18. Ps. 107:17-22.
19. Ps. 107:23-32.
20. Ps. 107:43.
21. J. Fischer & Brother, No. 9124, SATB.
22. Early American Moravian Church Music, No. 17. The H. W. Gray Company, Inc.
23. Rev. 5:11-13.

"HOW THE GREAT GUEST CAME"

We have attempted to point out in the previous services of worship that there is, not one way of presenting an idea, but several. The next two services are both based upon a poem by Edwin Markham, "How the Great Guest Came," (from *The Shoes of Happiness, and Other Poems.* Used by permission of Mr. Virgil Markham). The first service uses the original poem as part of a shorter service of worship that could be presented for a departmental assembly. The second service is a paraphrase of the poem and includes a service of worship as part of the dramatization. Music suggested for the services can be interchanged.

The setting for each service is the same, and includes a cobbler's bench, a stool, a table, and a bench. Costuming should be kept simple, but the use of bright-colored peasant clothing is desirable. Properties needed are a loaf of wheat bread, a pitcher of milk, honey, and evergreen boughs to decorate the bare room. In the first service, these decorations are in place at the beginning of the dramatization; in the second service the set is decorated as part of the action.

Both of these services can be presented by children from fourth grade through junior high. Separate rehearsals can be scheduled for the principal characters, the speaking choir, and the singing choir, thus necessitating only one or two complete rehearsals. The finished production could be presented for a parents' program or a Childrens' Day program.

FIRST SERVICE

Prelude: " Cathedral Fugue " [1]   Bach

Hymn: " O Master, Let Me Walk with Thee " " Maryton "

Poem: " Swinging Toward the Light " [2]

Anthem: " Be Thou My Vision " [3]   Arr. by Gordon Young

Scripture: Matthew 25:34-40

POETIC DRAMA: " How the Great Guest Came "

Narrator:

Before the cathedral in grandeur rose
At Ingelburg where the Danube goes;
Before its forest of silver spires
Went airily up to the clouds and fires;
Before the oak had ready a beam,
While yet the arch was stone and
        dream —
There where the altar was later laid,
Conrad, the cobbler, plied his trade.

(*Neighbors enter.*)

Speaking Choir (Girls' Voices):

It happened one day at the year's white
        end —
Two neighbors called on their old-time
        friend;
And they found the shop, so meager
        and mean,

171

Made gay with a hundred boughs of
  green.
Conrad was stitching with face ashine,
But suddenly stopped as he twitched a
  twine:

Conrad:

"Old friends, good news! At dawn to-
  day,
As the cocks were scaring the night
  away,
The Lord appeared in a dream to me,
And said, ' I am coming your Guest to
  be!'
So I've been busy with feet astir,
Strewing the floor with branches of fir.
The wall is washed and the shelf is
  shined,
And over the rafter the holly twined.
He comes today, and the table is spread
With milk and honey and wheaten
  bread."

(*Neighbors exit.*)

Narrator:

His friends went home; and his face
  grew still
As he watched for the shadow across
  the sill.
He lived all the moments o'er and o'er,
When the Lord should enter the lowly
  door —
The knock, the call, the latch pulled
  up,

The lighted face, the offered cup.
He would wash the feet where the
spikes had been,
He would kiss the hands where the
nails went in,
And then at the last would sit with him
And break the bread as the day grew
dim.

(*Beggar enters.*)

Speaking Choir (Boys' Voices):
While the cobbler mused, there passed
his pane
A beggar drenched by the driving rain.
He called him in from the stony street
And gave him shoes for his bruisèd feet.

(*Beggar exits; Crone enters.*)

Speaking Choir (Girls' Voices):
The beggar went and there came a
crone,
Her face with wrinkles of sorrow sown.
A bundle of fagots bowed her back,
And she was spent with the wrench
and rack.
He gave her his loaf and steadied her
load
As she took her way on the weary road.

(*Crone exits; Child enters.*)

Speaking Choir (a few girls' voices):
Then to his door came a little child,
Lost and afraid in the world so wild,

In the big, dark world. Catching it up,
He gave it the milk in the waiting cup,
And led it home to its mother's arms,
Out of reach of the world's alarms.

(*Exit Child and Conrad. Conrad returns immediately.*)

Narrator:

The day went down in the crimson
   west
And with it the hope of the blessed
   Guest,
And Conrad sighed as the world turned
   gray:

Conrad:

" Why is it, Lord, that your feet delay?
Did you forget that this was the day? "

Narrator:

Then soft in the silence a Voice he
   heard:

Voice (*The effect of the voice should be as from a great
distance*):

"Lift up your heart, for I kept my
   word.
Three times I came to your friendly
   door;
Three times my shadow was on your
   floor.
I was the beggar with bruisèd feet;
I was the woman you gave to eat;
I was the child on the homeless street! "

Hymn: " Spirit of God, Descend Upon My Heart "

                                      " Morecambe "

SOURCES

1. G. Schirmer, Inc.
2. Georgia Harkness, in Morrison, *Masterpieces of Religious Verse*, No. 1489.
3. Neil A. Kjos, Ed. 5254, SATB.

SECOND SERVICE

Introit: " Jesus, Kneel Beside Me " [1]   " Eudoxia "

Minister: O come, let us worship and bow down: let us
kneel before the Lord our Maker. God is a Spirit: and
they that worship him must worship him in spirit and in
truth.

Singing Choir: O Lord, open thou our eyes, that we may behold wondrous things out of thy law. [2]

Speaking Choir: Then the King will say to those at his right
hand,

Solo: " Come, O blessed of my Father, inherit the kingdom
prepared for you from the foundation of the world;

Speaking Choir (Group 1): For I was hungry and you gave
me food, I was thirsty and you gave me drink,

Speaking Choir (Group 2): I was a stranger and you welcomed me, I was naked and you clothed me,

Speaking Choir (Group 3): I was sick and you visited me,
I was in prison and you came to me."

Solo: Then the righteous will answer him,

Speaking Choir: " Lord, when did we see thee hungry and
feed thee, or thirsty and give thee drink? And when did
we see thee a stranger and welcome thee, or naked and
clothe thee? And when did we see thee sick or in prison
and visit thee? " And the King will answer them,

Solo: " Truly, I say to you, as you did it to one of the least
of these my brethren, you did it to me." [3]

Anthem: " All Glory Be to God on High " [4]   Bach

Narrator: " As you did it to one of the least of these my
brethren, you did it to me." How true that was of one
who lived here many years ago!

> Before the cathedral in grandeur rose
> At Ingelburg where the Danube goes;
> Before its forest of silver spires
> Went airily up to the clouds and fires;
> Before the oak had ready a beam,
> While yet the arch was stone and
>   dream —
> There where the altar was later laid,
> Conrad, the cobbler, plied his trade. [5]

SCENE I

*(The choir moves to one side and exits as the curtains open
to reveal Conrad sitting at his cobbler's bench.)*

Speaking Choir:
> Stitch, stitch, stitch, stitch, stitch, stitch,
> In and out with the awl and twine,
> In and out with the awl and twine,
> Stitch, stitch, stitch, stitch, stitch, stitch.

Conrad:
> I sing as I stitch, I stitch as I sing,
> I made good shoes which are fit for a
>   king,
> I have pride in my work and I try to do
> The very best job I can do for you. [6]

I stitch and stitch and stitch, working on shoes all day long. But today I don't mind. I'm so happy. What a wonderful day this is! Even though my shop looks bare, I can be happy. But perhaps I should do something about this bareness. I know — I'll call some of the children and ask them to help me gather some pine boughs. That will make the place a little more festive. And the pine always smells so good. (*Puts down shoe.*) I must hurry and get the children before they start for school. (*Goes to door and calls.*) Hello, hello, my good friends. Who will come and help me? Come and help your good friend Conrad. (*Conrad goes in and sits down and speaks.*)

> The sun is up, the bird's in flight,
> God has watched over me through the
>   night
> And now my heart with happiness
>   thrills
> And gladness my being fills.
>
> Thank you God for the morning light,
> Thank you God for the silent night,
> Thank you God for the bird in flight
> And for good friendship true.[6]

Gretel: Good morning, friend Conrad. How bright the day is!

Nancy: And all the world is glistening. It is so refreshing.

Gretel: We are all so happy. It is good to be alive.

All Children: Good morning, friend Conrad. What can we do for you?

Conrad: It is so good to see you this morning. Your faces look so happy. Yes, I do want you to do something for me, but first, sing me a song — the one that is my favorite.

Elise: The one that tells about the importance of having good shoes?

Conrad: Well, if you want to put it that way.

Heidi: But of course. You must put it that way. You can't enjoy walking unless you have good shoes.

Gertrude: What are we waiting for? Let's sing.

Song: " The Foot Traveler." [7]

Conrad: That was so beautiful that I scarcely feel I can ask you for anything more, and I would be content to listen to your singing all day, but I do need something.

Nancy: Well, tell us and we will see what we can do for you.

Conrad: Last night, I had a dream. In the dream the Lord appeared to me and told me he was coming this very day to be my guest. Now my poor shop is so bare that I would like to find some flowers and branches to make it more beautiful. Will you help me?

All Children: Of course, let's begin now.
(*The children and Conrad go out, joining the choir in singing the refrain of " The Foot Traveler."*)

(*Curtain.*)

SCENE 2

(*The bare room has been beautified by flowers and branches. Conrad is seated at his bench, working, as the curtain rises. Two women neighbors enter.*)

Conrad: Good morning, my good neighbors.

Neighbor 1: Good morning, Conrad.

Neighbor 2: Good morning, cobbler Conrad.

Conrad: What a wonderful morning it is!

Neighbor 1: And what makes you say that? It certainly hasn't been a good morning for me. First, the baby spilled the pitcher of milk all over the table. Then I burned the porridge when I went to clean the milk up. After that, the cat got up on the table and sat on the bread. Just one thing after another.

Conrad: I'm sorry to hear that you had so many difficulties.

Neighbor 2: You haven't heard anything until you hear what happened to me. My poor husband was sick all night, and I scarcely got any sleep at all. Then the dog hurt his paw, and when I went to see what the trouble was, the ungrateful beast bit me. I was so frightened that I jumped back and hit the table, sending the dishes onto the floor. And you say that it is a wonderful morning?

Conrad: It's a wonderful morning for me, good neighbors. I had a wonderful dream last night, and the Lord spoke to me to tell me he was coming to be my guest.

Neighbor 2: It certainly must have been a dream. Nothing like that could possibly happen.

Neighbor 1: And I see you've gone to a lot of trouble already — just for nothing. All these branches and flowers. Just a lot of extra work. Will you never learn? If you were my husband, I would soon put you in your place.

Neighbor 2: And I would too. It is useless to talk with you when you have such silly notions in your head. I can see we'll get little sympathy here, so let's be off. Good day, Conrad.

Neighbor 1: Good day.

Conrad: Ah, me. If only they would think less of themselves and more of others. But it is not for me to judge them. I try to live my life as best I can and give thanks always for all the good gifts God has given to me.

(*Choir begins to move onto the stage, humming the tune of "Thank Thee, God."* [8])

Conrad: How ungrateful we all are for the good gifts that are around us and that we so seldom see: the trees, the grass, the wind; water and stars; and the friendship that we have with one another.

Choir: "Thank Thee, God." [8]   Vulpius

(*Choir exits, humming tune. Conrad sits at his bench, his head bowed. The humming is punctuated with a cry of "Cobbler" which increases in intensity.*)

Beggar: Cobbler! . . . Cobbler! . . . Cobbler!

Conrad (*looks around*): Did someone call me? Perhaps it is the Lord coming to visit me.

Beggar: Cobbler! Cobbler! Be kind to me. Be good to me. Come, help me.

Conrad: Someone is calling. Wait! Wait! I shall be there. (*Rises and goes to door. Opens it and sees an old man standing there, his feet bound with rags.*) Come in, my friend. Let me bring you a chair so that you can rest your tired body.

Beggar: You are so very kind. Your next-door neighbors would have nothing to do with me. Wouldn't even open the door.

Conrad: They have had a hard day, but they really aren't so bad. Do not be disturbed by them, for you have found a friend here. You are indeed a sorry sight. First, let me get you some shoes. You came to the right place for those.

Beggar: For shoes I would be very grateful. It is no easy task to walk on the cobblestones with only rags to protect my feet.

Conrad: And you must have a cloak. I'll fetch one from the other room. (*Conrad goes out, and as he does, the beggar leaves.*) And here is a warm cloak — what? No one here? And he needed this cloak too. I'll put it here in case he comes back.

(*Conrad goes back to his bench and begins work. He sings " The Cobbler's Song." [6] As he finishes, the voice of a beggarwoman is heard.*)

Beggarwoman: Pity, take pity on me, good friend. I am so tired. I have carried these bits of wood all the way from the forest. I have had little to eat, and I must rest a while before I go any farther. My body is so tired. And my stomach is so empty.

Conrad: Come in, good woman. You are welcome here. Let me take your bundle of wood. Sit down and rest.

Beggarwoman: You are so kind. I have asked others for help, but they only turn me away from their doors, or send their dogs to nip at my heels. I mean no harm. I try to go about my business and not ask much of others. All I want is a place to rest.

Conrad: You have found it here. The chair is not the softest, but it is here to be used. And while you are resting, let me get you some bread to eat. It will give you strength to continue your journey. (*Goes to table and cuts some bread.*)

Beggarwoman: You are very kind. There are few who would be so good to such an old woman.

Conrad: I do not have much to offer, but what I have is yours. (*Gives her the bread.*)

Beggarwoman: My thanks to you, dear friend. This will indeed give me strength. And now I must be on my way.

Conrad: Let me help you with your bundle of fagots. At least I can carry it to the edge of the village.

Beggarwoman: You are indeed a true friend and Christian.

(*They go out.*)

(*Curtain.*)

SCENE 3

(*The curtains open to show Conrad sitting at his bench. He is humming "The Cobbler's Song."* [6] *A child appears at the open door.*)

Child: Oh me. Oh poor me. Where am I going? Where have I been? I do not know where I am, where I was, or where I will be.

Conrad: Wait, child. I will help you find your way.

Child: Can you help me? Can you help me find my way home? Can you show me where my mother and father live?

Conrad: Come here, child. I can try to find your home. First, tell me about yourself. Where were you going?

Child: I was trying to find my home. I was with my family as we went from our uncle's house up on the mountain to our house here in the valley. I began to chase butterflies and to gather nuts and flowers, and soon I was farther and farther away from my family. Then I felt hungry, but I found some berries and nuts in the forest. Soon it was dark, and I was frightened. I knew I was lost.

Conrad: Did you try to call your mother and father? Perhaps they would have heard you.

Child: I called and called, but only the echo of my own voice answered me. I started to cry, and began to run through the forest. Suddenly I came to a large meadow, and as I looked up, I saw the friendly stars twinkling in the sky. I remembered a song that we sing at home, and I sang it: "Can You Count the Stars?" [9]

Conrad: And you weren't afraid, because you remembered that God is watching over all the children in the world?

Child: That made me feel good inside, and I sat down on the soft grass and soon was fast asleep. When I wakened, I could see this village in the distance, and I began to walk here.

Conrad: You must be very hungry. Let me get you some bread and milk. Then we will go and find your mother and father. (*Exits.*)

Child: I'm glad I came here. The cobbler is so kind.

Conrad (*Enters*): Here is something for you to eat. While you are eating, tell me what your house is like.

Child: It isn't large, and it stands a little higher than the houses around it, so that it looks over the roof tops in the valley. Father has some goats. He built a small house for them that looks like a little castle, with a tiny flag on the top.

Conrad: And there are many flowers and trees around the house. And bright-red window boxes with snow-white flowers blooming in them. Is that not right?

Child: Yes, but how did you know?

Conrad: I pass it many times when I go up the mountain to get leather. It will not be long until you are home.

Child: You are so kind. But why do you do all these things to help me?

Conrad: It is because of the love which is in my heart. Listen. (*The choir offstage sings " Our Beautiful Earth."*)[10]

Conrad: Let us go now. I will take you to your home. (*They go out and the curtain falls.*)

SCENE 4

(*Some time has passed, and the shades of evening have come. Conrad is sitting at his bench as the curtain opens.*)

Conrad: The day has almost passed, and the Lord has not come. I was sure that he spoke to me last night. Why is it, Lord, that your feet delay? Did you forget that this was the day?

Voice (*The effect of the voice should be as from a great distance*):

Lift up your heart, for I kept my word.
Three times I came to your friendly
door;

Three times my shadow was on your
floor.
I was the beggar with bruisèd feet;
I was the woman you gave to eat;
I was the child on the homeless street! [11]

*(Choir enters, humming tune of "Now Woods and
Fields Are Sleeping," and stands behind Conrad. The beg-
gar, the woman, and the child come in and sit in front of
Conrad.)*

Choir: "Now Woods and Fields Are Sleeping." [12]

"Innsbruck"

Voice: As you did it to one of the least of these my brethren, you did it to me.[13]

Choir: "Lord, Let Us Now Depart in Peace." [14]   Mueller

(Curtain.)

SOURCES

1. *The Hymnal* (1933), Hymn 494. Presbyterian Board of
Christian Education.
2. *Ibid.*, No. 22, p. 468.
3. Matt. 25:34-40.
4. *Anniversary Collection of Bach Chorales,* No. 1. Schmitt,
Hall & McCreary Company.
5. Edwin Markham, "How the Great Guest Came." Used by
permission of Virgil Markham.
6. In the original production, these words were set to music
composed by the junior choir.
7. *Songs Children Like,* p. 19. Association for Childhood Education International, 1954.
8. Edith Lovell Thomas, *The Whole World Singing,* p. 121.
9. *Anthems for the Junior Choir,* Book 3.

10. Thomas, *op. cit.,* p. 41.
11. Markham, *op. cit.*
12. *The Hymnal* (1933), Hymn 505.
13. Matt. 25:40.
14. *Anthems for the Junior Choir,* Book 1.

THE DOOR OF GOD

The following service of worship is an attempt to translate into rhythmic movement the story of the prodigal son. Although a service using rhythmic movement is not usual in the church, this medium offers an endless variety of meanings. Historically, movement has been used for centuries in the worship of God. We read in the Old Testament that David danced before the Ark, and those who went in procession to the Temple on festival days doubtless moved rhythmically. We must remember that God speaks not only through men's voices, but also through their actions.

Those who participate in the rhythmic choir should wear flowing robes to enhance the grace of their actions. The skirts should end about mid-calf so that there is no danger of tripping. Although the dancers are essentially interpreting individually the meaning of the story, this interpretation should be minutely worked out so that each dancer knows what the others are doing. It is certainly desirable that the members of the rhythmic choir feel the moods of the story and convey these feelings in a meaningful way. Any variations which are desired should grow out of early rehearsals and should be incorporated into the total well in advance of the final presentation so that the entire service achieves unity.

The following service can serve as a suggestion for the interpretation of other parables through the use of rhythmic movements, and perhaps a trilogy of parables could be worked out.

In portraying any sequence with a rhythmic choir, it must be remembered that we are not pantomiming the action but attempting to interpret the action with symbolic movement.

It is also desirable that the musical background interpret the action. Certain selections have been suggested for use in the service. These selections cannot be given in entirety, but must be cut and spliced, augmented and abbreviated in order to portray accurately the meaning of the words. It would be even better to have the organist improvise or compose original music for the presentation.

Organ Prelude

PROLOGUE

Speaking Choir:

> Draw in the latchstring, lad, and close
> the door,
> Lest those who faint without from toil
> and pain
> Shall rob thee of thine own too meager
> store.
> Can one poor crust sustain those fam-
> ished forms?
> Can one poor shelter save them from
> the storms?
> And surely those who wait and hope in
> vain
> Shall turn and rend thee when thou
> hast no more,
> So — draw in the latchstring and close
> the door.

Solo:

> Such is the world's advice,
> But — there was One who flung it open
> wide —
> And he was crucified.[1]

Voice (*from the narthex of the church*): Truly, truly, I say to you, I am the door of the sheep. All who ever came before me are thieves and robbers; but the sheep did not heed them. I am the door; if any one enters by me, he will be saved, and will go in and out and find pasture.[2]

EPISODE I: THE DOOR TO THE WORLD

Organ: "Suite Gothique" (*Introduction*)   Boellman

(*The father, dressed in rich robes, walks slowly down the aisle, followed by his two sons. As they reach the chancel, twelve women, in flowing robes enter and form a semicircle around the three. They indicate, with their joined hands reaching upward, the closeness and security of the walls of a home. They show partial disintegration of this closeness by dropping hands and slowly sinking to the ground. As they do this, the speech choir begins.*)

Speaking Choir: There was a man who had two sons; and the younger of them said to his father, "Father, give me the share of property that falls to me." And he divided his living between them.

(*The younger son entreats his father, bowing before him and reaching out to him. The father bestows on the son his share of the treasure, while the older son turns his back and walks away.*)

Speaking Choir: Not many days later, the younger son gathered all he had and took his journey into a far country, and there he squandered his property in loose living.

Organ: "Fileuse"   Dupré
      "Nazard"   Langlais

(*The younger son begins the journey with quick steps.
Along the road to the far country, he is besieged by the
rhythmic choir, whose members entice him as individuals
and as small groups. He willingly gives what he has, and
this is received greedily by his new-found friends. They all
join hands and circle at an increasing tempo until they fall
exhausted.*)

Speaking Choir: And when he had spent everything, a great
famine arose in that country, and he began to be in want.
So he went and joined himself to one of the citizens of that
country, who sent him into his fields to feed swine. And he
would gladly have fed on the pods that the swine ate; and
no one gave him anything.

(*The younger son attempts to rise and to pull the others
with him. They will have nothing to do with him, and
crawl slowly away from him. Though he seeks to go after
them, they push him away, then suddenly leave him alone.
He rises, dejected, questioning, and scarcely knowing
which way to turn. He moves from one side to the other
in a frenzied search. At last a richly dressed man appears,
to whom the son attaches himself. The rich man sends the
prodigal son to feed his swine. The son enacts movements
which represent his groveling in the troughs of the swine,
seeking his food from their leftovers. His former friends
pass him by, looking at him haughtily. He sinks to the
floor at stage left and remains motionless.*

EPISODE II: THE DOOR TO THE FATHER

Organ: " Aria "   Peeters

Speaking Choir: But when he came to himself he said,
" How many of my father's hired servants have bread

enough and to spare, but I perish here with hunger! I will
arise and go to my father, and I will say to him, 'Father, I
have sinned against heaven and before you; I am no longer
worthy to be called your son; treat me as one of your
hired servants.'"

(*The son slowly rises to a sitting position, then suddenly
stands upright, as if he has just come to his senses. He sees
his father and his older brother at stage right surrounded
by the secure walls. Resolutely he begins his journey home,
stopping occasionally to lift his hands in prayer to God.
When he has almost completed his journey, he stops and
kneels down.*)

Speaking Choir: And he arose and came to his father. But
while he was yet at a distance, his father saw him and had
compassion, and ran and embraced him and kissed him.
And the son said to him, "Father, I have sinned against
heaven and before you; I am no longer worthy to be called
your son."

(*The father leaves the security of his walled home and goes
out to meet his son, lifting him from his kneeling position,
but the son bows down before his father; again he is lifted
up.*)

Speaking Choir: But the father said to his servants, "Bring
quickly the best robe, and put it on him; and put a ring
on his hand, and shoes on his feet; and bring the fatted
calf and kill it, and let us eat and make merry; for this my
son was dead, and is alive again; he was lost, and is found."
And they began to make merry.

Organ: "Suite Gothique" (Finale)   Boellmann

(*The father brings the rhythmic chorus to the center of the
chancel. They surround the father and the son with joined*

hands and begin to circle around them. Others come to join them, and there is gaiety as the rhythmic choir weaves in and out around the father and son. As they continue to make merry, the older son appears, looks at the merry-making, and turns his back on the group.)

Speaking Choir: Now his elder son was in the field; and as he came and drew near to the house, he heard music and dancing. And he called one of the servants and asked what this meant. And he said to him, " Your brother has come, and your father has killed the fatted calf, because he has received him safe and sound." But he was angry and refused to go in. His father came out and entreated him, but he answered his father, " Lo, these many years I have served you, and I never disobeyed your command; yet you never gave me a kid, that I might make merry with my friends. But when this son of yours came, who has devoured your living with harlots, you killed for him the fatted calf! "

(*The father leaves the merrymaking and tries to entreat the older son to come in, but he refuses. He begins to walk away with slow steps, his father coming after him. The rhythmic choir has arranged itself around the younger son in attitudes of thanksgiving. The father stops as the older son continues to walk into his own far country.*)

Solo: Son, you are always with me, and all that is mine is yours. It was fitting to make merry and be glad, for this your brother was dead, and is alive; he was lost, and is found.[3]

(*The father reaches out toward his departing son, then turns and stands beside the younger son. As the lights are dimmed, a voice from the narthex of the church is heard.*)

EPILOGUE

Voice: Behold, I stand at the door and knock; if any one hears my voice and opens the door, I will come in to him and eat with him, and he with me. He who conquers, I will grant him to sit with me on my throne, as I myself conquered and sat with my Father on his throne. He who has an ear to hear, let him hear what the Spirit says to the churches.[4]

Hymn: " O Jesus, Thou Art Standing "

"St. Hilda (St. Edith) "

Voice: The Spirit and the Bride say, " Come." And let him who hears say, " Come." And let him who is thirsty come, let him who desires take the waters of life without price. . . . He who testifies to these things says, " Surely I am coming soon." Amen. Come, Lord Jesus! [5]

SOURCES

1. Jessica Nelson North, from " A Warning," in *The Hymnal for Youth*, p. 375.

2. John 10:7-9.

3. Luke 15:11-32.

4. Rev. 3:20-22.

5. Rev. 22:17, 20.

VI

"I LOVE THY KINGDOM, LORD"

THE FOUR PROGRAMS IN THIS SECTION OF THE BOOK DEAL WITH the spreading of Christ's love at home and abroad. All these programs have been successfully presented by youth groups. In several churches their inspirational impact has acted as a catalyst for special projects that have been satisfactorily carried out. In this section we have tried first to show the historical background of the Christian church and then to demonstrate by word and action how we should respond in contemporary society.

"Love Made Manifest" is a very timely service. At the present period in the history of mankind, building is most necessary. There is a building of nations, of cities, and, most important, the building up of the spirits of those who are downcast. "A Christian World in Action" deals with two specters that continually haunt us — materialism and war. This dramatic presentation may be used almost any time in the year, for the struggle of man to be free is the continuing concern of all Christians, no matter when or where they may be living. "Christ and the City" is a service challenging youth to do something about the startling headlines of our newspapers — "Crowded City Housing a Cause of Juvenile Delinquency and Crime," or "Unemployment May Lead to Race Riots." A church in a large city used this program to start off a discussion for a social education and action meeting.

In several of the services it would be well to include a gallery of pictures or projected slides during the service. Excellent pictures and slides showing some of the areas of the world where there is great need can be obtained from the United Nations and from Church World Service. Because of the constantly changing problems and needs, we have not suggested specific pictures.

In presenting all these services, it is hoped that they will be used not only to point up a problem but so that the local church will see the need and take positive action. Responsible Christian citizens of the world are a necessity if we are to have a peaceful world.

THE LIVING CHURCH

The following service of worship is designed to show the continuing spirit of the church throughout the ages, and to tie our present-day congregations to the vast company of men and women who have witnessed to and worshiped God through the centuries. As a separate service it could be used, with the addition of a sermon or meditation, for a New Year's service, for Reformation Day, or for Pentecost. Certain substitutions would have to be made in hymns and anthems. Scripture, selected for the occasion, could accommodate the service to the particular day or season. The general plan that is presented on the following pages may serve as a guide for these special occasions. In the service as it is outlined, suggestions are made concerning pictures or slides of the local church, an open Bible, and a representation of the Creation. These pictures can be taken by someone in the church who is interested in photography as an art.

The service can also be used as an introduction to an anniversary celebration of a local church, or for the annual meeting of the congregation. If this is the intention, members of the local church can write additional narration telling of the work of that church in the community and in the world, and a committee in the church can be responsible for securing suitable pictures or slides to be used. In the local church it is especially important that we do not center upon ourselves, but that the heritage and world mission of the church be kept foremost.

Prelude: Improvisation on the hymn tune " St. Thomas "

(*During the prelude, the lights slowly go down.*)

Voice: In the beginning God created the heavens and the
earth. The earth was without form and void, and darkness
was upon the face of the deep. . . . And God said, " Let
there be light "; and there was light.[1]

(*During the above narration, a slide representing the Creation is projected. For this purpose, a photograph of clouds
may be used effectively.*)

In the beginning was the Word, and the Word was with
God, and the Word was God. He was in the beginning
with God; all things were made through him, and without
him was not anything made that was made. In him was
life, and the life was the light of men. The light shines in
the darkness, and the darkness has not overcome it.[2]

(*During the above narration, a slide of the open Bible is
projected.*)

Narrator 1:
>   This beginning was centuries upon cen-
>   turies
>   Removed from where we now stand.
>   In that portion of eternity
>   Which we call time,
>   Our beginnings can find measurement
>   Only in decades;
>   But we are bound to time past
>   By that vast army of men and women,
>   Saints and martyrs,
>   Who have witnessed to the Word,

> And who have brought the church of
>   Christ
> From those beginnings down to us
>   today.

Narrator 2:

> Today, tonight,
> We seek to recapture
> A part of our past,
> Knowing full well
> That the past serves us
> Only as a challenge to
> Future betterness.
> So we bring to you
> The Living Church,
> Taking bits from here and there
> That will reflect a portion
> Of the years now past.

(*During the narration, the slide of* Salisbury Cathedral *from the Bishop's Garden (Constable)* [3] *is projected.*)

Singing Choir: " I Love Thy Kingdom, Lord " (Stanza 1)
                                                 " St. Thomas "

(*During the singing, the lights gradually come up. The choir continues humming throughout the following narration and then sings the remaining stanzas of the hymn.*)

Narrator 1:

> So much has come and gone
> That we must synthesize,
> Compress, abbreviate.
> We have no value scale
> Of what is best and least.
> True value to the church

Is that which causes her to
Wake and witness to her Lord.
Let us therefore witness
To the love we hold for Christ's own
    church;
Let us hear the call
To demonstrate our love.
We cannot be observers
Of the years now past;
We must be participants
In the years to come.

Singing Choir:

"I Love Thy Kingdom, Lord" (Stanzas 2 to 5)

"St. Thomas"

*(In keeping with the text, and for variety, the third stanza
may be cast in the minor key.)*

Narrator 1:

Built upon a rock,
The church now stands
Stalwart and unrelenting
Against the onslaught of modern rivals.
Her faith has been defended,
Her being has been protected
By the words and prayers
Of men through the centuries.

Singing Choir: "Now Praise We Great and Famous Men" [4]

"Ach Gott und Herr"

Narrator 2:

Though centuries have passed,
We are still bound
To the heartfelt utterances
Of David, servant and king.

Voice 1: Let us pray.

> Out of the depths I cry to thee, O Lord!
>> Lord, hear my voice!
> Let thy ears be attentive
>> to the voice of my supplications!
> If thou, O Lord, shouldst mark iniquities,
>> Lord, who could stand?
> But there is forgiveness with thee,
>> that thou mayest be feared.
> I wait for the Lord, my soul waits,
>> and in his word I hope;
> my soul waits for the Lord
>> more than watchmen for the morning,
>> more than watchmen for the morning.
> O Israel, hope in the Lord!
>> For with the Lord there is steadfast love,
>> and with him is plenteous redemption.
> And he will redeem Israel
>> from all his iniquities.[5]

Narrator 2:

> Christians the world over
> Are bound together
> By the prayer that Jesus Christ
> First taught to his disciples.
> Now let us bind ourselves
> To his world-wide church
> As we pray his prayer together.

Congregation: The Lord's Prayer

Narrator 2:

> These words of Christ
> Have bound the church together:
> They have inspired those in the early
> church
> And those in the present day
> To give glory and honor to our Lord
> Jesus Christ.

Singing Choir: " Of the Father's Love Begotten "
                                      " Divinum Mysterium "

Narrator 1:

> Such voicing of love and praise
> Was a part of the early church.
> So too were confessions of sinfulness.
> Recognizing the city of men,
> And the City of God,
> One of the church's great leaders
> Prayed for a right spirit within himself,
> And history has projected this prayer
> To us today.

Voice 2: " Grant me, even me, my dearest Lord, to know
thee, and love thee, and rejoice in thee. And if I cannot do
these perfectly in this life, let me, at least, advance to
higher degrees of perfection every day. Let the knowledge
of thee increase in me here, that it may be full hereafter.
Let the love of thee grow every day more and more here,
that it may be perfect hereafter; that my joy may be great
in itself and full in thee. I know, O God, that thou art a
God of truth; O make good thy gracious promises to me
that my joy may be full. Amen." [6]

Narrator 2:

> Although all sought to worship
> God and Christ,
> There were some who felt
> That a revival of true faith was needed.
> Though burning was the lot of Hus,
> His faith in Christ and in the purity of
>   the church
> Overcame all fears of this world.

Singing Choir: "Jesus Christ Our Strong Salvation"

Hus-Dickinson [7]

Narrator 1:

> The breach was made by Luther.
> Great faith in Christ was his —
> The faith that just men live by.
> His prayer in words,
> Both read and sung,
> Show forth his trust
> In God and Christ.

Voice 3: "I give thanks to thee, my Heavenly Father, through Jesus Christ, thy dear Son, that thou hast this day so graciously protected me; and pray thee to forgive me all my sins and whatever wrong I have done, and graciously keep me through this night. For I commend myself, my body and soul and my all, into thy hands. Thy holy angel be with me that the evil one have no power over me. Amen." [8]

Hymn: "A Mighty Fortress Is Our God"

"Ein' feste Burg"

Narrator 2:

Through the centuries
Have marched the men of God:
Prophets and apostles,
Saints and martyrs,
All intent upon the sustaining
Of the living church.

Singing Choir: " I Love Thy Kingdom, Lord " (Stanza 1)
" St. Thomas "

Narrator 1:

And some, out of love for God's church,
Found their way to this place;
Gave of themselves,
Of their time and their talents,
To build this church.

(*Pictures of local church are projected. Additional narration and other pictures of the local church may follow.*)

Narrator 2:

But no matter how great or small,
No matter how many or few,
We are not the living church
Until we identify ourselves with the
past
And with the world-wide mission of
Christ's body.

Singing Choir:

" From Greenland's Icy Mountains " (Stanzas 1 and 3)
" Missionary Hymn "

Narrator 1:

This is ultimately the challenge that we
face:

That the witnessing church of Christ
Must reach out to the whole earth.
" The future depends on what we do,
What the world-wide church does;
How deep in Christ,
How widespread are ecumenical mis-
sion and relations.
We have one future;
What will it be?
Will Christians of ' the whole inhab-
ited world '
Keep watch with Christ and pray?
Or will we sleep and wake up too late?
Rise up!
The crisis of the future is here!
The hour of the future is now! " [9]

Narrator 2:

But do not only listen to these words;
Do not think only this night of the
church in this town,
And the work of the church in the
world.
This is something which requires
The day-by-day commitment
Of people like you and me.
Study;
Pray daily;
Teach children that they may know.

(*The following covenant may be projected on the screen,
or copies can be made available to the congregation as part
of the printed service.*)

Covenant with us this night
As we dedicate ourselves anew.

Congregation:

> We covenant this night with God and
> this assembled congregation
> To begin anew our work for the church
> of Jesus Christ.
> Let us not absolve ourselves from serv-
> ice to him
> Because we have served his church in
> past years;
> Neither let us work for the glory or
> honor that men shall give,
> But let us, with faith and determina-
> tion,
> Give of our lives, our material wealth,
> Our abilities, our knowledge,
> In joyful service
> To the King of Kings.

Hymn: " Rise Up, O Men of God "   " Festal Song "

Benediction

SOURCES

1. Gen. 1:1-3.
2. John 1:1-5.
3. The American Library Color Slide Company, No. 3341.
4. *Anthems for the Youth Choir,* Book 1.
5. Ps. 130.
6. Augustine.
7. Sacred Choruses, No. 239. The H. W. Gray Company, Inc.
8. Martin Luther.
9. *We Have One Future.* Commission on Ecumenical Mission
and Relations, The United Presbyterian Church U.S.A. Used by
permission.

A CHRISTIAN WORLD IN ACTION

This service of worship stands as a challenge to the youth of today and tomorrow to work for a Christian world. It can be used effectively for a youth conference or rally to point up the task that Christians have in the world. Because of its implications for the world mission of the church, it could be used during Lent in connection with the " One Great Hour of Sharing " appeal. It also could be used for the church's recognition of United Nations Day. Surely there is a place in the church calendar for a recital of the moving words of some of our great Christian leaders, such as John Wesley, George Fox, and Henry Knox Sherrill.

This service can be presented in the chancel or in the social hall. It can be embellished by the use of authentic costumes, tableaux of the needy of the world, and selected slides secured from Church World Service. It would be very effective if the singing and the speaking choirs could be composed of members of different races, or if the choirs could be costumed to represent various nationalities.

The form that the production takes will depend upon the type of group before which it is being presented and the physical equipment available. Although it is suggested that a speaking choir carry much of the script, this does not need to be a permanently organized group, but can be formed by a nucleus from one of the singing choirs or from a youth group. It is also possible to use a reading quartet rather than a speaking choir.

Processional: " God of Our Fathers, Whose Almighty Hand "   " National Hymn "

*(During the processional hymn, flags of all nations and
the Christian flag are carried down the aisles and grouped
at the front. The Christian flag is in the honored position.)*

Speaking Choir:

> "The old order changeth, yielding
>   place to new,"
> And we must face the problems of to-
>   day
> With steadfast heart, unclouded mind,
> Press toward the goal, forgetting all be-
>   hind
> In which we've failed; seek out a way
> To conquer evil and uphold the right.
> Each generation has its foes to fight.

Solo 1:

> What do we face?

Speaking Choir:

> Two enemies, at least, uprear their
>   heads:

Solo 2:

> Mammon — almighty dollar, with its
>   power;

Solo 3:

> And Mars, the deadly serpent of the
>   hour.

Speaking Choir:

> No washing of our economic hands
>   will be enough;
> No sudsing of our governmental face;
> We must strike deeper, to the very root,
> If we would be a truly Christian race.

> The " group called Christian " must its
>   ardor don
> And mass its power against the force of
>   wrong,
> United, earnest, counting all else dross,
> Willing to pay the price — yea, even a
>   cross!

Anthem: " O God of Earth and Altar " [1]   Redman

(During the anthem, the lights are dimmed and spot-lights pick up the grouping of flags. During the last stanza, the Christian flag is lifted up.)

Speaking Choir:

> Good Christian folk they call them-
>   selves,

(Several groups of people come down the aisle and take their places in the front pews.)

> Who almost every Sunday fill a pew,
> Yet by cowardly silence rendered mute;
> They fail — they fail to give the Christ
>   his due.

Solo 1:

> Ah yes! They fail — they fail to realize
> (Or else they do not care)
> That in their hands the nascent future
>   lies,
> That they can make it either dark or
>   fair.

Speaking Choir:

> That choice, my friend, is one we dare
>   not shirk.
> On which side stand you, now, in glib
>   array?

Women:

> God or Mammon?

Men:

> God or Caesar?

Speaking Choir:

> On which your trust you stay?
> The future calls in piteous, pleading
> tone,

Solo 1:

> Oh, give me Life, a life of holy verve,
> A life in which the cross of Christ is
> throned.

Speaking Choir:

> Choose ye; choose now, this day, whom
> ye will serve.

Narrator:

> The old order must change if we are
> to have
> What is supremely needed:
> A Christian World Order.

Skeptic (*rising from a front pew*):

> What do you mean, a Christian World
> Order?
> I'm sick of just words!
> What *is* a Christian?

Narrator:

> Well, an answer to your question
> Is a pretty large order.[2]

Listen, and hear what men through the
ages have said.
John Calvin, writing in the fifteen hun-
dreds, said this:

Calvin: (*The spotlight picks up Calvin as he takes his place
on the pulpit.*) The moral law is composed in two leading
articles, of which one simply commands us to worship
God with pure faith and piety, and the other enjoins us
to embrace men with sincere love — this law, I say, is the
true and eternal rule of righteousness, prescribed to men
of all ages and nations, who wish to conform their lives
to the will of God. For this is his eternal and immutable
will, that he himself be worshiped by us all, and that we
mutually love one another.[3]

Narrator: And George Fox, the founder of the Society of
Friends, wrote:

Fox (*speaking from the pulpit*): Our weapons are spiritual,
not carnal, yet mighty through God to the pulling down
of the stronghold of Satan, who is the author of wars,
fighting, murder, and plots. Our swords are broken into
plowshares, and spears into pruning hooks. Therefore we
cannot learn war any more, neither rise up against nation
or kingdom with outward weapon.[4]

Narrator: John Wesley, the great leader of the Evangelical
Revival and the founder of the Methodist Church, began
his work as a result of his own conversion experience. In
his *Journal,* on the date of May 24, 1738, he tells us of this
experience:

Wesley (*speaking from the chancel steps*): In the evening
I went very willingly to a society in Aldersgate Street,
where one was reading Luther's preface to the Romans.

About a quarter before nine, while he was describing the change which God works in the heart through faith in Christ, I felt my heart strangely warmed. I felt I did trust in Christ, Christ alone, for salvation; and an assurance was given me that he had taken away my sins, even mine, and saved me from the law of sin and death.[5]

Narrator: And Henry Knox Sherrill, the first president of the National Council of Churches, has recently said:

Sherrill (*speaking from the pulpit*): We talk of democracy in world terms. Democracy emphasizes the worth and the values of the individual. But apart from a faith in God, of what eternal significance is personality? In the faith of the Christian is to be found the inspiration of the finest and best in our civilization. It is time that we think of the church in large terms of intelligence, interest, and support. For if the Christian evangel be true, here is the greatest of all causes given by God into the hands of men. Upon this rests all other efforts for the attainment of peace and righteousness.[6]

Narrator: [7] Does that answer your question, Mr. Skeptic? Christianity really does make a difference, both individually and internationally.

Skeptic: Well, that *sounds* good, but all the Christians in the world haven't been able to stop war or bring lasting peace yet! What are they doing worth fussing about?

Narrator: If you can wait a few moments, maybe some others can show you what has happened, and what we are doing and can do to help.

(*The Skeptic subsides, mumbling to himself. The lights go down until all is darkness. With staccatolike insistence comes the cry of the speaking choir.*)

Speaking Choir:

> War! War! War! War!
> Is there no loyalty but death?
> Must blood and gore
> Be used to fertilize our fields
> Forevermore?
> Cannot our patriots have life
> By word and deed?
> Will not their ministrations serve
> The human need?

(Lights gradually come up.)

Solo 1:

> Then give us peace,
> But peace with honor.

Speaking Choir:

> " Peace with honor " was the cry
> Of statesmen long since gone,
> And " Peace with honor " is the cry
> That ever must live on.

Solo 2:

> But what is Honor, O ye men
> Who'd plunge the world in bloody
>   strife?
> Hast not each pledged before just God
> To cherish and protect his wife
> And child — the emblem of his love?

Solo 3:

> But what about those other wives and
>   youth
> You doomed to war's dark horrors rife?

Have they no right to justice, mercy,
    truth?
Does not God look in pity from above
Upon the struggling masses of the
    world,
While selfish men the hounds of hate
    unleash,
And thunderbolts lie waiting to be
    hurled?

Speaking Choir:

If Honor means, O selfish man,
That for thine own unholy ends thou
    canst
Wreak havoc on poor, helpless babes,
And suffering, desolation spread
O'er fair earth's wide domain,
Then Honor is not worth its name,
And Peace with Honor best is dead!
If Honor means that men shall live
As brothers — true, unselfish, kind,
The world — a Brotherhood of Man,
Then Peace shall dwell with human-
    kind.

Skeptic:

Yeah, that's the kind of war we've had;
But what is real Peace?

Speaking Choir (*continuing as if not interrupted*):

Then said the student,
Speak to us of peace.
And the teacher answered, saying,

Solo 1:

> Peace is not absence of war, but a new
>   kind of war;
> It is the war of faith against fear;
> It is the war of love against hate.
> Peace is not the shuffle of a hobo's shoes
>   in the dust,
> But the feel of rich earth against the
>   toes of a farmer
> Following his plow.
> Peace will grow only through the
>   plowed fields of sacrifice and self-
>   giving.
> You will not find peace caged in the
>   narrow walls of your houses, nor
>   walking on the paved streets of
>   your cities;
> But peace will find you, if you are
>   worthy, in the fiery passion of sun-
>   rise,
> The roaring of a great river,
> Or the whispering of willows in the
>   spring evening.
> You shall not find peace with folded
>   hands,
> But Peace shall find you at the end of
>   the day
> If you have given and suffered and bled,
> If you have worked and forgiven and
>   loved,
> And become yourself a part of life's
>   innermost secret.

Skeptic:

> That's what I call Peace, too!
> But what about right now;
> The hungry and cold war orphans can't
>   eat words!

(*The lights are dimmed.*)

Speaking Choir:

> We planned an ultramodern home,
> But a Belgian girl whispered,

Solo 4:

> " I have no home at all."

Speaking Choir:

> We dreamed of a country cottage for
>   happy weekends,
> But an Arab refugee kept saying,

Solo 5:

> " I have no country."

Speaking Choir:

> We decided on a new cupboard,
> But a child of China cried out,

Solo 6:

> " I have no cup."

Speaking Choir:

> We wanted an immense freezer
> For storing quantities of food,
> But across the water came the cry,

Solo 7:

> " I have no food at all."

Speaking Choir:

> We ordered a new car for the pleasure
> of our loved ones,
> But a war orphan murmured,

Solo 8:

> " I have no loved ones."

Solo: " O Brother Man " [8]

(During the music, pictures of the needy of the world are projected.)

Narrator:

> We know that our task is only begun;
> Our work must go on and on.
> Can you see now what being a Christian means?

Skeptic:

> This makes some sense.
> Those fellows don't just sit and talk.
> They're not like these Sunday Christians
> Who go to church one day and forget
> the next —
> The guys with the limousines and plush offices
> Who dole out the dough.

Narrator:

> Silence!
> Look around at the drudgery of life
> And let your conscience speak to your heart.
> Where do you stand today?

Speaking Choir:

> In honor with the men who raise your
> food?
> The men who slave by furnace, tool,
> and net?
> What have you done for them?
> You've paid your paltry pennies as a tax
> To build their schools, their roads, their
> churches, and their homes.
> You have been kind.

Solo 1:

> You think you've paid for them?
> Their sweat, their pain,
> Perhaps their tears and blood?

Speaking Choir:

> Come down to earth, you high and
> mighty ones,
> And smell the stench of men who die
> for you.
> Not on the battlefields in hero's glory,
> But in the factory, farm, and common
> street.
> They died from work,
> Incessant, killing work,
> With muscles bulging till the vessels
> broke
> And spilled their blood upon the bench,
> the forge.

Solo 2:

> You hang your head and pray?

Speaking Choir:

> Could you expect
> Almighty God to hear your pagan
>   prayers,
> While you reject the men
> Who feed your mouth?
> Who clothe your back?

Solo 3:

> Hang your head in shame and listen
> As their voices speak from darkness,
>   warm and sultry.
> Listen on in deep, unending silence.

Speaking Choir:

> Man, if you would be free,
> Release yourself,
> Give up your tight hold
> Upon your little self.
> Become an instrument of Good;
> Share with thy fellow man.

Skeptic:

> Fellow man? Who's he?

Narrator:

> Every man is your fellow man!
> Be he red, white, yellow, or black,
> He should be free.

Skeptic:

> He should be free?
> Why, we're all free!

Narrator:

Are we?
What of the millions of people, just
    people,
Living and working together,
Walking the freedom road:
Black and white,
Jew and Gentile.
For these, this freedom is the same.

Skeptic:

What do you mean,
The same for black and white,
For Jew and Gentile?

Speaking Choir: We hold these truths to be self-evident, that
all men are created equal; that they are endowed by their
Creator with certain inalienable rights; that among these
rights are life, liberty, and the pursuit of happiness.[9]

Narrator:

This is the struggle of man to be free.
This is the task of all mankind,
Without end.

Speaking Choir:

This is the task of all Christians!

Anthem: " A Hymn of Freedom "[10]   Thiman

SOURCES

1. Novello & Co., Ltd., M.T. 1182 (The H. W. Gray Company,
Inc.). If this is not available, the words, set to the hymn tune
" Llangloffan " may be used.

2. The poetic selections beginning with "The old order changeth, yielding place to new" are from a service of worship created by the Greater Philadelphia Christian Youth Group.

3. From *Guide for Worship Services, Youth Week, 1955*, p. 6. Published for the United Christian Youth Movement by the National Council of Churches.

4. *Ibid.*, p. 6.

5. *Ibid.*, p. 7.

6. *Ibid.*, p. 7.

7. The poetic selections from here to the end are from a service of worship created by the Greater Philadelphia Christian Youth Group.

8. Sung to the hymn tune "Welwyn," or the anthem setting by Geoffrey Shaw may be used (Novello & Co., Ltd., No. 1147).

9. From the Declaration of Independence.

10. The H. W. Gray Company, Inc., No. 1683.

LOVE MADE MANIFEST

The Christian church is continually seeking ways in which it may demonstrate to others the love of God that is in our hearts. In the last quarter century, work camps have become a means for demonstrating this love, and while only a small proportion of the Christian church can take part in these work camps, it is well that the rest of us know what great service they give. Such a service of worship as the one that follows can be used to interpret the work camp idea, to interest young people in this kind of project, and to gain support for work camps from the material gifts of others.

The service can be presented effectively in either the chancel or the church social hall. At the rear of the stage or chancel there are graduated tiers on which the singing choir stands. Members of this choir may be dressed as historical men and women who have helped build the Kingdom of God on earth. Their presence and the words they sing are symbols of the support the church gives to the young work campers. The speaking choir occupies the front of the stage or chancel. They are dressed in work clothes, carry tools with which they work, and are seated on wooden boxes and nail kegs.

At the beginning of the service, the stage is dark. During the call to worship, the lights gradually come up as the choir sings " Worship," by Shaw.[1] Following the invocation, and just before the presentation by the speaking choir, the anthem " Be Strong," by Fryxell,[2] is sung. Other anthems may be used during the service according to the wishes of the director. These are suggested as possibilities: " Rise Up, O

Men of God," by Walter Shaw,[3] and " Built on a Rock," by Christiansen.[4]

Narrator 1: Hear the words of Nehemiah the son of Hacaliah as he spoke to the returned exiles.

Narrator 2: " You see the trouble we are in, how Jerusalem lies in ruins with its gates burned. Come, let us build the wall of Jerusalem, that we may no longer suffer disgrace." And I told them of the hand of my God which had been upon me for good, and also of the words which the king had spoken to me.[5]

Narrator 1: And they said, " Let us rise up and build." So they strengthened their hands for the good work.[6]

Narrator 2: From this point in time in the history of the world, from those days in 444 B.C., the people of God have been building together, uniting in common endeavors, seeking to overcome some of the obstacles that had been set before them,

Narrator 1: And knowing that " as the mountains are round about Jerusalem, so the Lord is round about his people." [7]

Narrator 2: So in the portion of time that we choose to call the modern world, there were those who looked beyond themselves; who looked far out across the world darkened by clouds of political unrest, war, hatred, insecurity, poverty, and a host of other spectres which were dividing the world and her people.

Narrator 1: There were those who became conscious of the needs of a world torn by conflicting views of the nature and destiny of man. There were those who refused to sit in complacency, shut out from the reality of the world by windows of stained glass and walls of brick and stone. There were those voices who kept on saying:

Speaking Choir (Light Voices): "Let us rise up and build." Let us rise up with the help of God and build again what has been broken down. Let us rise up and build homes for the homeless, houses of worship for those who have none.

Narrator 1: There were also those who added:

Speaking Choir (Medium Voices): "Let us rise up and build." Let us rise up with the help of God and build what has been broken down. Let us rise up and build anew the spirits of those who are downcast, bring hope to the hopeless, and love to those who have learned to hate.

Narrator 2: They were few in number at first. They were so few that their voices were not heard except in isolated places, but their ideas were not easily put down. Their voices became stronger and were translated from active ideas to accomplished purposes. And they kept on saying:

Speaking Choir (Dark Voices): "Let us rise up and build." Let us rise up with the help of God and build again what has been broken down. Let us make manifest our Christian love. Let us practice our Christian faith, our Christian witness, our Christian citizenship, our Christian fellowship, our Christian outreach.

Narrator 1:

> O brother man, fold to thy heart thy
>   brother;
> Where pity dwells, the peace of God is
>   there;

> To worship rightly is to love each other,
> Each smile a hymn, each kindly deed a
> prayer.

Narrator 2:

> Follow with reverent steps the great ex-
> ample
> Of him whose holy work was doing
> good;
> So shall the wide earth seem our
> Father's temple,
> Each loving life a psalm of gratitude.[3]

Narrator 1: It was more than twenty years ago that the work camp idea was given its first serious trial in the United States. From that work camp in western Pennsylvania, the idea has spread, until today work camps are held in our own country as well as in American-sponsored camps abroad.

Narrator 2: Work camps in the mountains of Colorado; work camps in Egypt; work camps on the Dakota plains; work camps in the mountains of Italy; work camps among the orchards of Michigan; work camps in the countryside of southern France.

Narrator 1: And so we have built Agape in Italy, a migrant center in Michigan, College Cevenol in France, a church in Colorado.

Narrator 2: And the going hasn't been easy. When you consider what a work camp really is, you know that it's not a chance to see the world.

First Voice: A work camp is an opportunity to give service that will meet some human need. And it's putting into action our Christian principles by our physical labor.

Second Voice: A work camper receives no pay. He participates in the work camp because his desire for service to his fellow man is greater than his desire for monetary payment. Further, each work camper shares in the expense of the work camp by paying his own way.

Third Voice: But a work camp is not all work. There is the opportunity to learn more about our brother Christians, to see the needs of the world, to be a member of a close fellowship of those united in a common endeavor, and to grow in faith through the experience of meditation and prayer and Bible study.

Narrator 1: A work camp is based on these three principles, but it is not principles that make a work camp. It is not the work itself, it is not the fellowship alone, it is not the Bible study or the prayer or meditation.

Narrator 2: It is not the individuals who make up the work camp. It is not those who benefit from the work camp. It is not the completed project. It is instead the many intangible things which come to those who give and to those who receive. It is their own spiritual growth in its fullest sense that makes them realize that they are not a privileged group of people but a part of the community of Christians. Listen to what they say.

First Voice: Ye olde callouses are returning! Gravel had to be scooped for the cement mixer, and it really keeps us all busy to keep things going. It takes three wheelbarrows of gravel, one bag of cement, and three buckets of water for one mixerful of concrete.

Second Voice: Some church members donated fish for our supper, and a woman from the village brought us a bushel

of canned goods. The community has truly responded and
has been very gracious and generous. This is one of the
many ways in which love is made manifest, for we campers
can see the community responding to our presence, and
we, too, are gaining a lot from our association with them.
In fact, I feel that we gain a lot more than we ever give.

Third Voice: For the months following the war, there was
hatred in my heart toward the German people. Then I
participated in a work camp in my own land of France.
I made friends quickly with the young people from
America who were there. It was not so easy to make
friends with a German youth, even though the others told
me he was not to blame for the war. Then one morning
the German youth led our devotions. He read: " A new
commandment I give to you, that you love one another;
even as I have loved you, that you also love one another.
By this all men will know that you are my disciples, if
you have love for one another." [9]

Narrator 1: And on and on could go the stories of those
whose participation in a work camp has been the cause
for their growth in the Christian life. Theirs was an experience which showed forth the working of the spirit of
Christ. Though tired and sometimes discouraged at the
end of the day, they could still say:

Speaking Choir:
> But they who wait for the Lord shall
>   renew their strength,
>   they shall mount up with wings like
>   eagles,
> they shall run and not be weary,
>   they shall walk and not faint.[10]

Narrator 1: And the people said, Let us rise up and build. So they strengthened their hands for the good work. And not only did they strengthen their hands, but they strengthened their spirits as well. They strengthened the bonds of Christian love among all peoples of the world.

Speaking Choir (Light Voices): It is not enough that we give our money alone so that the work of Christ will go forward in all the world. It is not enough that we seek to grow in the knowledge of the Christian faith. It is not enough that we think of others and ourselves as one fellowship in Christ.

Speaking Choir (Medium Voices): It is not enough that we give our physical strength to rebuild what has been broken down. It is not enough that we work under hardships to finish a job. It is not enough that we sacrifice so that we can participate in such an experience.

Speaking Choir (Dark Voices): There is never enough that we can do. We do not glory in our accomplishments but rather become dissatisfied that there is so much that could be done. We do not look for praise nor seek to do that which will call attention to ourselves.

Speaking Choir: Rather do we seek to show forth the love which is in our hearts. Through our work, through our living together, through our spirit of brotherhood, through the deepening of our Christian faith and service do we desire to make our Christian love manifest. " That we being rooted and grounded in love, may have power to comprehend with all the saints what is the breadth and length and height and depth, and to know the love of Christ which surpasses knowledge, that we may be filled with all the fullness of God." [11]

Narrator 1: Lord, make me an instrument of your peace; where there is hatred, let me sow love; where there is injury, pardon; where there is doubt, faith; where there is despair, hope; where there is darkness, light; and where there is sadness, joy.

O Divine Master, grant that I may not so much seek to be consoled as to console; to be understood, as to understand; to be loved, as to love; for it is in giving that we receive, it is in pardoning that we are pardoned, and it is in dying that we are born to eternal life. Amen.[12]

SOURCES

1. Novello & Co., Ltd., No. 1147, SATB (The H. W. Gray Company, Inc.).

2. *Anthems for the Youth Choir,* Book 1.

3. Lawson-Gould 794-25, SATTBB. G. Schirmer, Inc.

4. St. Olaf Choir Series, No. 104. Augsburg Publishing House.

5. Neh. 2:17-18a.

6. Neh. 2:18b.

7. Ps. 125:2.

8. John Greenleaf Whittier.

9. John 13:34-35.

10. Isa. 40:31.

11. Eph. 3:17-19 (adapted).

12. St. Francis of Assisi.

CHRIST AND THE CITY

Although the majority of Americans live in cities, there are thousands, both in the cities and in rural areas, who know little about the problems of the church in the city. This service of worship is designed to point up some of those problems and to make Christians of this country aware of their mission to the city. The service that follows can be used as an introduction or as a conclusion to the study of the city by the local church.

The action of the service takes place in front of a city sky line. The background is white, with outlines of buildings in black. The stage is dimly lighted in blue. The speaking choir should be at one side of the stage, and the narrator, soloists, and "Voices" at the other side. The Voices represent individuals who have come to the city, and should be costumed appropriately. They may walk to stage center in a disorganized procession, symbolizing the thousands who come to the city to seek something they may not find. The Voices represent the following: Voice 1, a college-trained professional who wants to get ahead; Voice 2, a sharecropper who has been driven out by "farm factories"; Voice 3, a youth who wants a career in art, music, or on the stage; Voice 4, a Maine villager who wants a better chance for his children; Voice 5, a mountaineer who hears of the demand for labor in Detroit.

It is hoped that the use of this service will result in an increased understanding of the city and in some steps that can be taken by the local church to aid the church in the city.

Prelude

Hymn: " Where Cross the Crowded Ways of Life "
                                        " Germany "

CHORAL READING

(*The cast consists of a narrator and an interracial speaking
choir representing the voices of people living in any cosmo-
politan city. The characters noted in the introduction and
mentioned in the script may be chosen from the speaking
choir.*)

Narrator: Listen! Listen to the voices in the crowded ways
of the city — the voices of the bewildered, in need of
Christ. Are you alert? Can you hear?

Speaking Choir:
>We dwell in your community.
>We are the voices of your community.
>We are the strangers living around you.
>We worship in your church.
>Can you help us?
>We have lost our way.
>Where is the way? Can you tell us?

Narrator: Jesus said, " I am the way, and the truth, and the
life; no one comes to the Father, but by me." [1] He came to
seek and to save that which is lost.

Speaking Choir:
>We are the weary voices in your city.
>Here, we are hungry.
>Here, we are cold, sick, discouraged.
>We are the weary voices crying out:
>" Who will help us? What bright voice
>>will bring us hope? "

Narrator: " Happy is he whose help is the God of Jacob, whose hope is in the Lord his God, who made heaven and earth, the sea, and all that is in them; who keeps faith for ever; who executes justice for the oppressed; who gives food to the hungry." [2] Jesus said, " Come to me, all who labor and are heavy-laden, and I will give you rest." [3]

Speaking Choir:
> Voices of every city cry in despair!
> What of our old age, our unemployment?
> We are afraid.
> We are the widows, the handicapped, the blind.
> Many have cried. Is our cry in vain?
> Darkness is over us. We are afraid.

Narrator: " The people who sat in darkness have seen a great light, and for those who sat in the region and shadow of death light has dawned." [4] Jesus said, " I am the light of the world; he who follows me will not walk in darkness, but will have the light of life." [5]

Speaking Choir:
> We are the dwellers of cities,
> Of crowded ways —
> Struggling for life,
> Searching for truth.
> Hope is our need today.
> Love is our goal.
> Peace! Give us peace, we pray.

Narrator: Jesus said: " Peace I leave with you; my peace I give to you; not as the world gives do I give to you. Let not your hearts be troubled, neither let them be afraid." [6]

" Behold, I stand at the door and knock; if any one hears my voice and opens the door, I will come in to him and eat with him, and he with me." [7]

Voice 1: So I came to the city because I wanted to get ahead.

Echo Voice: " Everyone who exalts himself shall be humbled."

Speaking Choir: Get ahead . . . make money . . . buy a car, a bigger car, a better car . . . make money . . . money . . . get ahead!

Voice 2: But I can't find a place to live. We haven't much money. I can't pay the rent they ask. I can't find a place . . . I can't find a place.

Voice 3: I want a big car; I want a big house; I want a big job.

Echo Voice: " A man's life does not consist in the abundance of his possessions."

Voice 1: But I want to get ahead . . . if I can find a place to live . . .

Speaking Choir: Crowded housing . . . crowds . . . noise . . . three families in one room . . . forty thousand in a trailer camp . . . no room . . . crowds . . . crowds . . . the *city*.

Voice 4: My children have no place to play . . . we can't pay the rent in a better street . . . it's so noisy here . . . but I want to get ahead . . .

Voice 5: They told me I could find a job here . . . I've got to find a job . . . I've *got* to.

Speaking Choir: Noise . . . noise . . . crowds . . . no place to play . . . no place to rest . . . children playing on pavements . . . babies sleeping on pavements . . . no room . . . no room . . . get ahead . . . get ahead . . . the *city*.

Echo Voice: " What does it profit a man, to gain the whole world and forfeit his life? "

Voice 5: I've looked up and down the streets for a familiar face . . . you can be awfully lonesome in a crowd . . . and the subways roaring . . . and the old people . . . and the children . . . I'm afraid here!

Speaking Choir: Roar of subways . . . roar of machines . . . crowds . . . crime . . . noise . . . alone . . . afraid . . . get ahead . . . the *city*.

Echo Voice: Go tell it in the city, that Jesus Christ is Lord.

Speaking Choir: Yes! Go tell it in the city, tell it in the city . . . Jesus Christ is Lord.[8]

Hymn-Anthem: " Thy Kingdom Come, O Lord "

" St. Cecilia "

POEM: " THY KINGDOM COME "

Solo 1:

> Thy Kingdom come
> And quickly, Lord!
> For Life is a tempestuous sea,
> Where storm-winds beat unceasingly
> And drive us oft away from thee.

Speaking Choir:

> So, day by day,
> We ever pray —
> " Thy Kingdom come!
> Thy Kingdom come! "

Solo 2:

> Thy Kingdom come!
> Lord, till it comes,
> We are but voyagers who roam
> With straining eyes amid the gloom,
> And seek but cannot find our home.

Speaking Choir:

> So, day by day,
> In faith we pray —
> " Thy Kingdom come!
> Thy Kingdom come! "

Solo 3:

> Thy Kingdom come!
> For when it comes
> Earth's crying wrongs will be redressed,
> And man will make his chiefest quest
> The Peace of God which giveth rest.

Speaking Choir:

> So, day by day,
> In hope we pray —
> " Thy Kingdom come!
> Thy Kingdom come! "

Solo 1:

> Thy Kingdom come!
> Ah, grant us, Lord,
> To see the day when thou shalt reign
> Supreme within the hearts of men,
> And Love shall dwell on earth again!

Speaking Choir:

> For that, thy Day,
> We ever pray — [9]

(During the above lines, the choir hums " Lead On, O King Eternal.")

Congregation *(in unison)*: The Lord's Prayer
   Our Father who art in heaven,
   Hallowed be thy name.
   Thy kingdom come, thy will be done,
   On earth as it is in heaven.
   Give us this day our daily bread;
   And forgive us our debts, as we forgive
      our debtors;
   And lead us not into temptation,
   But deliver us from evil.
   For thine is the kingdom and the power
      and the glory,
   Forever. Amen.

Hymn: " Lead On, O King Eternal "   " Lancashire "

SOURCES

1. John 14:6.
2. Ps. 146:5-7.
3. Matt. 11:28.
4. Matt. 4:16.
5. John 8:12.
6. John 14:27.
7. Rev. 3:20.
8. *Adult Guide on " The City,"* by Ione Catton, pp. 10–12. Friendship Press, 1954. Used by permission of the publisher.
9. " Gentlemen — the King! " by John Oxenham in *The Hymnal for Youth*, p. 380. Used by permission.

BIBLIOGRAPHY

Anthologies of the Arts

Luccock, H. E., and Brentano, Frances, eds., *The Questing Spirit*. Coward-McCann, Inc., 1947.

Maus, Cynthia Pearl, *Christ and the Fine Arts*. Harper & Brothers, 1938.

—— *The Old Testament and the Fine Arts*. Harper & Brothers, 1954.

Ritter, Richard H., ed., *The Arts of the Church*. The Pilgrim Press, 1947.

Wagenknecht, Edward, ed., *The Story of Jesus in the World's Literature*. Creative Age Press, Inc., 1946.

Art

Bailey, Albert E., *Christ and His Gospel in Recent Art*. Charles Scribner's Sons, 1948.

—— *The Gospel in Art*. The Pilgrim Press, 1944.

Fleming, Daniel Johnson, *Each with His Own Brush*. Friendship Press, 1952.

Godfrey, F. M., *Christ and the Apostles: The Changing Forms of Religious Imagery*. The Studio Publications, Inc., 1957.

Hodgkin, Eliot, comp., *A Pictorial Gospel*. The Macmillan Company, 1950.

Ross, Marvin, ed., *The Life of Christ in Masterpieces of Art and the Words of the New Testament*. Harper & Brothers, 1957.

237

Audio-Visual

Audio-Visual Resource Guide. National Council of Churches, 1954.

Guide to Films. The Religious Film Association, 1954.

Choric Speech

de Banke, Cécile, *The Art of Choral Speaking.* Walter H. Baker Co., 1937.

Gullan, Marjorie, *Spoken Poetry in Schools.* Expression Co., 1931.

Keppie, Elizabeth Evangeline, *Choral Verse Speaking: An Avenue To Speech Improvement and Appreciation of Poetry,* Expression Co., 1939.

Swann, Mona, *The Approach to Choral Speech.* Expression Co., 1934.

Drama

Plays for Churches. National Council of Churches, 1960.

Eastman, Fred, *One-Act Plays of Spiritual Power.* Walter H. Baker Co., 1948.

Malcolmson, Anne, *Miracle Plays.* Houghton Mifflin Company, 1959.

Switz, Theodore, and Johnston, Robert, eds., *Great Christian Plays.* The Seabury Press, Inc., 1956.

Religious Drama, Vol. 1, M. Halverson, ed., 1957; Vol. 2, E. M. Browne, ed., 1958; Vol. 3, M. Halverson, ed., 1959. Meridian Books, Inc.

Music

Bailey, Albert Edward, *The Gospel in Hymns: Backgrounds and Interpretations.* Charles Scribner's Sons, 1950.

Dearmer, Percy, and others, *The Oxford Book of Carols.* Oxford University Press, Inc., 1928.

Morsch, Vivian Sharp, *The Use of Music in Christian Education.* The Westminster Press, 1956.

Wernecke, Herbert H., *Christmas Songs and Their Stories.* The Westminster Press, 1957.

Rhythmic Movement
Andrews, Gladys, *Creative Rhythmic Movement for Children.*
Prentice-Hall, Inc., 1954.
Sheehy, Emma Dickson, *Children Discover Music and Dance:
A Guide for Parents and Teachers.* Holt, Rinehart and Winston, Inc., 1959.
Taylor, Margaret Palmer Fisk, *The Art of the Rhythmic Choir:
Worship Through Symbolic Movement.* Margaret Palmer
Fisk Taylor, 30 N. College St., Athens, Ohio.

Theatrical Handbooks
Bailey, H., *The ABC's of Play Producing: A Handbook for the
Nonprofessional.* David McKay Company, Inc., 1955.
Bates, E., *The Church Play and Its Production.* Walter H.
Baker Co., 1938.
Eastman, Fred, and Wilson, Louis LeRoy, *Drama in the
Church: A Manual of Religious Drama Reproduction.* Samuel French, Inc., 1942.
Ehrensperger, Harold Adam, *Conscience on Stage.* Abingdon
Press, 1947.
Ward, Winifred Louise, *Playmaking with Children, from Kindergarten to High School.* Appleton-Century-Crofts, Inc.,
1947.

Worship
Coffin, Henry Sloane, *The Public Worship of God: A Source
Book.* The Westminster Press, 1946.
Hedley, George, *Christian Worship.* The Macmillan Company,
1953.
Underhill, Evelyn, *Worship.* Harper & Brothers, 1937.

PUBLISHERS' ADDRESSES

Abingdon Press (Methodist), 201 Eighth Avenue, South, Nashville 3, Tenn.

American Baptist Publication Society, 1701–1703 Chestnut Street, Philadelphia 3, Pa.

American Library Color Slide Company, Inc., 222 W. 23d Street, New York 11, N.Y.

Artext Prints, Inc., Westport, Conn.

Augsburg Publishing House (Lutheran), 426 S. Fifth Street, Minneapolis 15, Minn.

Augustana Book Concern, 639 38th Street, Rock Island, Ill.

Walter H. Baker Co., 569 Boylston Street, Boston 16, Mass.

M. Barrows & Company, Inc., 425 Park Avenue, S., New York 16, N.Y.

Boosey & Hawks, Inc., 30 W. 57th Street, New York 19, N.Y.

Canyon Press, Inc., Box 351, Bloomfield, N.J.

Chappell & Co., Inc., 609 Fifth Avenue, New York 17, N.Y.

Christian Education Press (Evangelical and Reformed), 1505 Race Street, Philadelphia 2, Pa.

Concordia Publishing House (Lutheran), 3558 S. Jefferson Avenue, St. Louis, Mo.

J. B. Cramer and Company, Ltd., 139 New Bond Street, London W. 1, England.

Farrar, Straus & Cudahy, Inc., 101 Fifth Avenue, New York 3, N.Y.

Carl Fischer, Inc., 56–62 Cooper Square, New York 3, N.Y.

J. Fischer & Brother, Main Street and Harristown Road, Glen Rock, N.J.

Harold Flammer, Inc., 251 W. 19th Street, New York 11, N.Y.

Samuel French, Inc., 25 W. 45th Street, New York 36, N.Y.

The Frick Collection, Fifth Avenue at 70th Street, New York, N.Y.

Friendship Press, 475 Riverside Drive, New York 27, N.Y.

Galaxy Music Corporation, 2121 Broadway, New York 23, N.Y.

The H. W. Gray Company, Inc., 159 E. 48th Street, New York 17, N.Y.

Harper & Brothers, 49 E. 33d Street, New York 16, N.Y.

Holt, Rinehart and Winston, Inc., 383 Madison Avenue, New York 17, N.Y.

International Art Publishing Company, 243 W. Congress Street, Detroit, Mich.

Neil A. Kjos, 525 Busse Highway, Park Ridge, Ill.

John Knox Press (Presbyterian U.S.), 8 N. Sixth Street, Richmond, Va.

The Macmillan Company, 60 Fifth Avenue, New York 11, N.Y.

The Metropolitan Museum of Art, Fifth Avenue at 82d Street, New York 28, N.Y.

National Council of Churches, 475 Riverside Drive, New York 27, N.Y.

New York Graphic Society, 95 E. Putnam Avenue, Greenwich, Conn.

Oestreicher's Prints Inc., 1208 Sixth Avenue, New York 36, N.Y.

Oxford University Press, 417 Fifth Avenue, New York 16, N.Y.

C. F. Peters Corporation, 373 Fourth Avenue, New York 16, N.Y.

The Pilgrim Press (Congregational Christian), 14 Beacon Street, Boston 8, Mass.

Theodore Presser Co., Presser Place, Bryn Mawr, Pa.

Religious Drama Society of Great Britain, 166 Shaftesbury Avenue, London, W.C. 2, England.

G. Schirmer, Inc., 609 Fifth Avenue, New York 17, N.Y.

Schmitt, Hall & McCreary Company, Park Avenue at Sixth Street, Minneapolis 15, Minn.

The Seabury Press, Inc. (Episcopal), 1 Fawcett Place, Greenwich, Conn.

Summy-Birchard Publishing Company, 1834 Ridge Avenue, Evanston, Ill.

The Viking Press, Inc., 625 Madison Avenue, New York 22, N.Y.

The Westminster Press (United Presbyterian), Witherspoon Building, Philadelphia 7, Pa.

GLOSSARY

Antiphonal singing — An arrangement of the choir into two separate choirs, whereby a dialogue in music is carried on by the choirs. This is achieved either by having one choir on one side of the chancel, and the other choir opposite them, or by having one choir in the chancel and the other in the gallery or balcony.

Apron — That portion of the stage which extends forward beyond the curtain line to the footlights. (Also called forestage.)

Balanced voices — A blending of varied tone colors of the speaking choir so that a range of voices from low to high, both in quality and pitch, is created. This may be comparable to the parts of a singing choir.

Border — A width of cloth hung above the scenery to conceal the upper part of the stage. There may be several of these borders, the one nearest to the footlights being referred to as the first border.

Border light — An overhead strip of lights parallel to the proscenium arch.

Chancel — The front part of the church proper, ordinarily reserved for the ministers and the choir.

Curtain line — The imaginary line on the stage that would be formed by the bottom of the drawn curtain. Also, the last line of dialogue.

Cyclorama — A smooth, curved surface of cloth often used to represent sky.

Dark voices — The voices of a speaking choir that make up the lower register, i.e., bass and baritone.

Dissonance — The sounding or playing together of tones that are out of harmonic agreement.

Downstage — The portion of the stage that is toward the footlights and mid-stage and parallel to the proscenium.

Drape — A long piece of cloth draped over the body to form a simple costume. It is usually belted with the same fabric. A head covering extending below the shoulders completes the costume.

Ensemble — Any combination of two or more performers, usually limited by the fact that each performer is assigned to a separate part. In an ensemble there should be no individual display of prominence, but each person functions as a member of a team.

Flat — A section of scenery made from a wood frame covered with cloth and joined to other frames to form the background for a set.

Gelatine — A colored piece of isinglass, or a cellophane-like substance, inserted in the frame of a spotlight to create varying effect.

Hand props — Those properties carried on stage by the actors.

Introit — A short choral composition used at the beginning of a service of worship.

Light voices — The voices of a speaking choir that make up the upper register, i.e., soprano.

Medium voices — The voices of a speaking choir that make up the middle register, i.e., alto and tenor.

Narthex — The vestibule of a church leading to the nave, or main body of the church.

Nave — The main body of the church and separate from the transepts and chancel.

Opaque projector — A projector that reproduces flat pictures or other plane-surface materials by means of reflected light.

Orchestration — The arrangement of material for the speaking choir, taking into consideration the mood of the selection. This includes arrangements for the total choir, semi-chorus, solos, and other combinations.

Proscenium — The structural meeting of stage and auditorium, especially referring to the frame around the stage.

Recorder — An instrument of the flute family which enjoyed great popularity during the sixteenth and seventeenth centuries.

Rheostat — An electrical device that controls the intensity of light so that there may be a gradual adjustment from very bright lights to complete darkness.

Royalties — The payment made to a publishing house for permission to present a play or pageant.

Sanctuary — In limited usage, that portion of the church proper in the vicinity of the altar; in many nonliturgical churches, the main body of the church.

Set piece — A piece of scenery that stands by itself and is in the acting area.

Solo part — In the speaking choir, an individual part, preferably selected from auditions, conveying the characterization that is desired.

Speaking choir — A group of balanced voices speaking and thinking as one.

Spotlight — A high-wattage bulb and reflector in a metal box which allows light to escape only through a condensing lens. This is used to highlight the stage and produces a circumscribed area of light.

Stage left — The part of the stage on the actor's left as he faces the audience.

Stage right — The part of the stage on the actor's right as he faces the audience.

Transept — The part of a cruciform church which crosses at right angles to the greatest length and between the nave and the apse or choir.

Tunic — A blouse or coat, usually belted, and extending to the hips or knees.

Upper stage — The rear half of the stage.

Wings — The side of the stage where the actors remain while off stage, and which is cut off from the view of the audience.

INDEX